The Power
of
Inner Guidance

The Power
of
Inner Guidance

Seven Steps to Tune In and Turn On

Pam Garcy, PhD

iUniverse, Inc.
New York Lincoln Shanghai

The Power of Inner Guidance
Seven Steps to Tune In and Turn On

iUniverse books may be ordered through booksellers or by contacting:

iUniverse
2021 Pine Lake Road, Suite 100
Lincoln, NE 68512
www.iuniverse.com
1-800-Authors (1-800-288-4677)

Because of the dynamic nature of the Internet, any Web addresses or links contained in this book may have changed since publication and may no longer be valid.

ISBN: 978-0-595-42240-1 (pbk)
ISBN: 978-0-595-86578-9 (ebk)

Printed in the United States of America

The information, ideas, and suggestions in this book are not intended as a substitute for professional advice. Before following any suggestions contained in this book, you should consult your personal physician or mental health professional. Neither the author nor the publisher shall be liable or responsible for any loss or damage allegedly arising as a consequence of your use or application of any information or suggestions in this book.

Care was taken to change details relating to identity of case examples to protect the confidentiality of individuals mentioned.

To my mother, Lucy, who was always there to guide me,

To my husband, Roger, who has continued to help me to grow with his patience and love,

and

In memory of my father, Donald, who reinforced my compassion for others and encouraged me to live life courageously.

Contents

Acknowledgments

An author may start a book alone, but like a child, it is raised by a village. I wish to offer many thank-yous, but I must start first with G-d, who has given me countless and abundant blessings throughout my life. Thank you for blessing me once again with the chance and ability to write this book, with the individuals who have shaped my thinking, with the experiences that led to the conclusions, and with the answers to my prayers along the way.

Thanks to my dear and hilarious husband, Roger, for giving me so much support, encouragement, laughter, and the best role model for winning I've seen. You truly are the wind beneath my wings and I will always love you enormously. Thank you to my adorable children, Brittany, Ethan, and Max, for understanding that Mommy had a book inside of her and that she had to take time to work on sharing it.

Thanks to my sister and soul mate, the Honorable Annie Garcy, who is always gently honest and loving to me. Annie, you have shown me a true example of ethical living and kindheartedness. There is none better than you. Thanks also to my mother, Lucy Garcy, for being my first teacher, for believing in me, and for telling me over and over to do something with my writing! Well, I guess it took me a while, but Happy Birthday! Thank you also to my big sister, Laura, for encouraging me to go to Mega and for inspiring me to be creative and to walk with determination upon my own path, like you. Thanks also to my father-in-law, Ron, and the rest of my family for their encouragement.

A person is often the sum of the people with whom they spend their time. While not all of my friends can be mentioned here, I want to thank each of them for contributing to my life and to this book in their own way. Special thanks go to my dear friends and supporters: Melanie, Kay, Ala, Beila, Karen, Andrea, Joanne, Amy, Carol, Debbie, Theresa, Shelly, Ethel, Cathy, and Maria. Each of you has played a specific and important part in the success of this project. Special thanks to my dear friend, best-selling author Teresa Bolen!

Heartfelt and abundant thanks also go to Jack Canfield, for writing *The Success Principles* and all of his other masterpieces, for telling me about Mega, and for graciously supporting my efforts with this book! Jack, your inspiration fanned my burning desire to write this book! Thank you for all you've done!

I would also like to thank the five greatest coaches in the USA, the coaches from Jack Canfield's *Success Principles,* for their wonderful help and wise guidance. Ken Porter was especially gracious during the creation of the first draft of this book. All of them helped me to write from my heart. Thanks, guys!

I would also like to thank Dr. Albert Ellis for his openness to my book, despite his recent illness. Dr. Ellis's Rational Emotive Behavioral Therapy has profoundly shaped my own thinking, not to mention my treatment of patients. I am thrilled that one of the greatest thinkers of our time was willing to take the time to review my work! Heartfelt thanks to John Minor, PhD, for encouraging me to approach Dr. Ellis.

I must also extend my appreciation to all those who helped in the publication and distribution of this book. Thanks to my first Web site designer, Steve Lillo, at Planet Link for stopping me from saying "if" and reminding me to say "when." Enormous thanks goes to Matt Bacak for teaching me how to get my book to those who need it, and to Alex Mendossian for helping me learn what my readers really need to know, and for helping me reach out through the Internet and teleseminars. Thank you to Mark Victor Hansen, who I first met at one of his Mega Book Marketing Universities, for his encouragement and wisdom, and for connecting me to pioneers in the field. Thanks also goes to other authors whom I've talked to along the way, for being generous with their time and encouragement: Stephen Chandler, *100 Ways to Motivate Yourself;* Susan Jeffers, *Feel the Fear and Do It Anyway;* Michael Edelstein, *Three Minute Therapy;* Barbara DeAngelis, *How Did I Get Here?;* Richard Paul Evans, *The Christmas Box;* John Kremer, *1001 Ways to Market Your Books;* Rick Frishman, *How to Get on Oprah and Other PR Secrets;* Jean Houston *The Possible Human: A Course in Enhancing Your Physical, Mental, and Creative Abilities;* and others.

Thank you to all of the folks at iUniverse who were involved in the publication of this book.

Thanks also to my graduate students at Argosy University, who were helpful in reading the book and providing feedback about it. Thanks also to the staff and teachers at my children's schools; without your support of my children, this book would not have been possible!

To my readers, thank you for being open to the part of you that was drawn to this book. Statistics show that many people buy books but don't read them. How sad! You were drawn to this one for a particular reason, so don't put it down until you get something out of it! Then, when you do, keep on reading it, because you're probably going to get something more within a few pages. If you simply begin to apply some of the positive actions you read here, you will start to experience new ideas and thoughts that lead to new actions and better life results. It is my belief that if you consistently apply what you learn in this book, and if you practice daily, you will not only experience relief, but will be on the road to transforming your life into one of purpose and passion. Let's make that happen!

DISCLAIMER

While this book will probably be very helpful for the vast majority of those who are drawn to it, as a psychologist, I have an ethical obligation to consider those who might not be ready to embark upon this journey. Just as you shouldn't embark upon a new exercise program before checking with your doctor, it is also important to get clearance before you embark upon a new mental/emotional journey. In that respect, I wish to inform you that this book assumes a basic level of mental fortitude and functional health. If you are severely mentally ill, have experienced ongoing hallucinations and/or delusions, or if you have been given a diagnosis of a delusional disorder, thought disorder, or any type of psychotic disorder, *please* ask your psychiatrist or psychologist for clearance before embarking upon this voyage. Thank you for doing this for yourself!

Part I
A Parable, A Paradox, and A Plan

Chapter One
The Two Brothers

The silhouette of a man graced the outline of a charcoal-colored mountaintop against a background of cerulean ocean and sky. In thinking posture, the man reviewed how he had arrived at this moment in his life. As he zipped his sweatshirt to ward off the coolness, he realized that it had been over twenty years since he'd sat on the stone seat beneath him; not since his graduation from high school had he returned. Now, at forty, he was revisiting this spot, questioning and uncertain, as though begging for answers about what went wrong.

So much had changed in his life. He remembered the events of the years that seemingly led up to his present way of life. He thought back to the pats on the back from his father and his mother describing him as a "gem." He recalled his wife calling him a "trooper" and his friend calling him a "great guy." He recalled the nauseous feeling that those words seemed to invoke within him, and the inseparable feelings of self-disdain and self-loathing that followed. Yet, he remained conflicted between wanting everyone to adore him and wanting to follow his own path.

As he sat watching the waves crashing violently on the rocks below, he pondered the choices he'd made in his life. He recalled his buddies telling him, "You should marry her. She's the prettiest girl you've ever dated."

He recalled a time when he was seven years old, when his father encouraged him, "One day, son, all this will be yours. You'll have it easy. You won't have to struggle like I did—you'll just walk right into partner." He remembered showing his mother a picture of a house in the mountains of Colorado, and how she easily had discounted him. "Honey, we figured you'd live in the villa we bought you so that you could be with us when you two lovebirds have children." As he listened to the water crashing and retreating, he suddenly felt flooded with the events that had brought him to his present reality.

Beginning to sob, his mind wandered to thoughts of his younger brother. He recalled how his friends would ask him about his younger brother, and he found himself defensively, though approvingly saying things like, "Well, he marches to the beat of his own drummer," or "That's just him." He recalled his secret intrigue as he would watch his brother move through life as though the world were there for his design, and as though he were immune to disapproval. Seemingly unaffected by the comments of others, his younger brother's self-reliance now consumed him; he couldn't understand how his brother could do the things he did, and he did not know how to simultaneously support and condemn such brazen autonomy.

Observing early in life that his older brother seemed to be fighting a losing battle, the younger brother recognized that he would be better off working toward his own ends, rather than vying for the approval of others. Indeed, the younger brother frequently met with disapproval; however, he recognized this as a part of life and accepted it. Because of this, unlike his older brother, he felt very comfortable making his own decisions and walking upon his own path. He chose his wife because she was the woman he felt most connected to, he chose his job because it was his passion, and he chose his place of residence because he felt at home and at peace there.

Both brothers lived lives that appeared fulfilling to those on the outside, carrying all of the accolades that they'd been raised to consider important. But secretly, the older brother was beginning to tire of the empty, silent yearning that had at first whispered to him, had eventually began to tug at him, and that now was beginning to pelt him like rocks thrown by schoolboys against glass windows of an abandoned house. He often sensed that there was something missing, and frequently turned to others for his answers. "What do you think I should do?" he asked his parents, his wife, and his friends. Somehow their directives were never as fulfilling as he'd hoped they'd be. At times when he turned to others, they would tell him to do things that he felt were out of sync with what he thought and felt. However, he did not want to upset or disappoint anyone, so he found himself bending and flexing to accommodate others in his world. If he thought that he was straying off track, he would quickly dismiss the idea. He would resign himself to the plans others had made for him, ignoring the urging feelings within.

All the while, the younger brother was busy pursuing dreams he'd always had, making new friends, taking on new challenges, and enjoying the fruits of these quests. He learned to turn away from doubt and discouragement, finding these to be unhelpful. He learned that if he kept his head, he could usually figure out a pretty good solution to his problems.

Now the older brother sat turning his head to the sky. "Why?" he asked the seagulls that flew in a *v* directly over him. He wondered why he was finding himself in the middle of the very conflicts he'd lived his life avoiding. His sobbing subsided, and he became quiet, breathing the crisp air that surrounded him.

Often, others in his life disagreed with each other; then, they'd each expect him to yield to their preferences. What was he supposed to do? Early in his marriage, his mother wanted him to have Thanksgiving at her house, while his wife wanted him to have it at their house. He felt extremely uneasy and did not know what to do. Inside, a voice suggested, "Let's have it somewhere altogether different, let's go to a cottage out of town, let's …" but before his own voice could offer further suggestions, he silenced it by yielding to the most powerful of the people in his life. His mother was so powerful to him, even though he was an adult with a wife, that this was the voice he often chose to listen to. His wife was filled with jealous disappointment much of the time. Again and again, conflicts emerged. He had to make choices about who to listen to.

"Why me?" he questioned, looking out in the distance as though the answer would magically write itself before him.

"You did this," a voice inside seemed to answer.

He recalled how he would walk around feeling anxious about what would happen next. The fear of disappointing others seemed like a vise around his neck, gripping him and holding him back. He remembered moments when he felt unhappy with his life, very disappointed in himself, but without knowing exactly why. The sadness of his existence felt like a heavy weight around his chest, pulling him down. When he did not have to go to work, he'd sometimes spend the whole day lying in bed and suffering; he did not want to get up and face his life because he could not understand how to improve it.

He had ignored his healthy inner voice for so long that he was often confused. Added to the depression and anxiety was his problem with anger. Sometimes, he found himself filled with rage that seemed to come from nowhere, like the time he was driving and found himself chasing another driver who had cut him off. Other times, he would wake up with nightmares in which he was trying to yell for help, but couldn't get the words out.

Over the course of many years of allowing others to dictate his life course, the older brother found that central relationships in his life were beginning to crumble. Those he'd tried most to impress had lost respect for him. At work, his own team often just told him what would happen, rather than including him in the planning. Moreover, his closest friends did not seem to trust or respect what he had to say, seeing him as a chameleon and a sheep. His wife eventually had enough of his instabilities and inabilities and decided that it was time for a trial separation. That was his wake-up call.

He knew his younger brother had faced challenges as well, especially that of criticism from others as he made the decisions that seemed to fit for him. In addition, his family sometimes tried to elicit guilt, telling him what he "should" do and discouraging his more shameless decisions. However, he found strength and persistence within himself, which allowed him to depart from their program for him.

As the man sat on his stone seat, he suddenly heard footsteps. Approaching him was his younger brother. Softly, the younger man climbed upon the cold, damp rock and sat next to the man. He looked around, saying, "What a view. I can see why you came here to think." He was concerned about his big brother, who had left a curious note about where he'd be but had not left a time that he'd return. He decided that just sitting next to him would be enough for now.

After several minutes of sitting together silently, the older brother turned to the younger and asked, "What do you think is going wrong with my life?"

"What's more important is what you think," the younger answered simply.

"I really don't know."

"Are you certain you don't know?"

After a moment, the older brother answered, "I just know that my life seems to be falling apart."

Although the younger brother felt a bit out of role in suggesting solutions to his older brother, he decided it was okay to offer some ideas. So he said, "Perhaps this is a turning point for you. Perhaps your time has finally arrived. Maybe you are ready to start guiding yourself."

"My time. Guiding myself. Hmmph."

"I think that you could start by learning to accept yourself for who you are and for where you are now. This is what it is. You've lived how you've lived. This is the outcome that has emerged," said the younger man.

"Yes, it is the outcome, but not the one I wanted."

"The past doesn't predict the future," said the younger. "So, let's look forward. What did you want?"

"I just wanted to be loved, that's all. I'm not sure where I went wrong."

"Do you think that maybe you wanted it a little too much? Maybe you wanted it so much from others that you forgot?"

"Forgot what?" said the older brother.

"Forgot that you cannot control others—even if you give them everything they ask of you, they still may not love you as you're demanding that they do. Forgot that you have interests and goals of your own. Forgot to pursue your dreams. Forgot that this is your life, and that you own the choices and the outcomes. Forgot to be true to your heart." The younger brother added a perfunctory, "Perhaps?"

The older brother, astonished by his brother's clarity and wisdom, looked at him with pause. "Yes—I forgot these things. You're right."

They sat in silence again, noticing the wispy cirrus clouds that streaked the sky. A seagull was dunking its head in the water, emerging with a shiny black fish, which it quickly gulped down.

The younger brother rapidly realized that his older brother had been dancing this dance for so long, he wasn't aware that there were other steps to take. "Look, I'm here to help you," he offered. "I know we're very different, but I believe your life can be much better than it is now—so much better that you won't even recognize it—if you're willing to do the work it takes."

The younger brother spoke from the heart. He knew that when he felt aligned with his purposes and goals, and that when he lessened his demands to preferences, he was better able to joyfully and energetically pursue that which absorbed him. Then, he was happier and had more of himself to share with those whom he loved. He found that, over time, his decisions often turned out to be beneficial for him and for those he loved. He had learned to make more well-informed, ethical, and rational decisions, and this led him to feel quite comfortable trusting himself to cope with whichever outcomes emerged. Sure, there were times when he made mistakes, lost money, and even lost so-called friends. However, because he worked to accept himself and others despite mistakes, he often learned great lessons from his defeat. Then, he was able to apply the lessons learned to other experiences.

The younger brother reached into his pocket. He pulled out a folded sheet of notebook paper upon which he'd scribbled the titles of several books. "These authors have given their wisdom away; they've shared it, and you can have it cheaply. Years of struggle, years of reading, and years of learning from mistakes have led to these books. I think they would help you on your journey for answers."

"Well, why not? What do I have to lose at this point anyway?" said the older brother, in a tone somewhere between discouragement and cynicism.

Recognizing his older brother's pain, the younger man knew that he would have to tread softly. However, he also knew that he could probably offer something of value. He did not need his brother to take it, but he would offer the tools as a gift.

The older brother knew his younger brother was sincere. He'd noticed how his younger brother could be very persistent, and he'd often admired this strength. There was something compelling about his younger brother's ability to stay the course; it seemed to lead to good life results. This was quite opposite the result that he himself had obtained in all his efforts to create a life of connection by bending and yielding.

"So, look at some of the titles. Do any appeal to you?" said the younger.

The older brother scanned the list for a couple of minutes. "Here's one, I think."

"Okay, hold on," the younger brother said. He got up and walked off. Twenty minutes later, he returned with a dog-eared copy of the book that his brother had chosen.

"I brought this for you. It will help you to return to yourself, and it will help you to refocus and move forward," the younger brother said, offering the book.

"What do you mean?" questioned the older brother, taking the book and looking at the cover.

"Well, you'll learn to take some time out, get by yourself, ask yourself whatever tough questions are bugging you, and give yourself a chance to pick a saner direction."

"To tell you the truth, it sort of freaks me out to do that."

"Why?"

"Well, I tried doing something like that once and I got so many thoughts all at once that I got confused. I started feeling panicky. I decided never to do that again. It's just, you know, uncomfortable!"

"That's fine. But maybe you're freaking yourself out because you don't understand the process of returning to yourself, and you're demanding that everything be clear all at once."

"Yeah, wouldn't you?"

"Well, it would be nice to get your answers quickly and to have everything go smoothly and easily. But I learned a long time ago that I couldn't make everything be as I wanted it to be all the time, and that it certainly took effort and work to reach my goals. Even so, I realized that I couldn't guarantee any specific outcome. There isn't any certainty except that you've been given *you* for now. So, even though I admit to liking the feeling of things being clear and guaranteed, I've given up on *needing* them to be."

"Yeah, but do you actually take time out and turn inward and all that?"

"I know it may sound kind of funny to you, but whenever I can, I do. Usually I like it, because I stay in touch with what I think is important, and I get a chance to clear my mind and refocus. But it isn't always perfect! So I've also learned that it is good for me to write stuff down and come back to it."

"What do you do when you come back to it?"

"I look at it and ask myself some specific questions about it. It helps me to evaluate my thoughts and to keep a healthier outlook."

"What do you ask?"

"Well, look, I think it would help you to read the book. Once you've read a little bit about this method, you'll know when to do what, and you'll have all the questions in front of you. I think you'll get the idea, because it is user-friendly. But in case you don't, I'll check in with you and we can discuss whatever you don't get."

"Okay, I guess I may as well. At this point, I feel so crummy that it doesn't matter anyway."

"So, you'll give up a few minutes of feeling crummy and read this?"

"Yeah," the older brother said, laughing and staring at the book. "Sounds a little deep for me ... but I may as well give it a try, if that's what you think. What the heck, right?"

"No, please don't read it because that's what I think. Read it because that's what you think."

"All right ... to tell you the truth, as I listened to what you were saying, that is what I started to think. I figure if you're into this and it is working for you, I may as well see what it's all about too."

"Now *you're* talking!"

Chapter Two
Freedom and Responsibility: Two Sides of the Same Coin

Welcome to a book that is here to help you to get back in touch with yourself, figure out the next steps upon your own path, recognize the possibilities in your life, get relief from your mental obstacles, and create a life that will exceed your present expectations! I am honored that you've been drawn to this book, and I hope that it serves you well. If you just reviewed the depiction of the two brothers, you might be wondering who they are and where they came from. Both brothers represent an amalgamation of patients I've seen (at various phases of treatment) as a clinical psychologist in private practice. You might also think of the older brother as a metaphor for your old ways of doing things, and the younger brother as a metaphor for the new ways you will learn in this book. Neither is perfect, but the younger brother is freer and passionately self-directed. This is ultimately what this book strives to help you to do for yourself: own and recognize your freedom, claim your right to release your passion, and courageously take responsibility for the journey.

I know what it is like to be in conflict about the direction of your life; decisions can become onerous when you recognize the responsibilities that escort your free choice. I faced some tough questions when I decided to stay home with my children for their early years instead of accepting seemingly exceptional career opportunities in my chosen field of psychology—and that's only one example. My heart told me to stay with my children and that, when the time was right, I would move to helping others. I cannot tell you how many times I've been glad I made the decision to be true to my own timeline for life, despite the short-term financial sacrifices.

We cannot always fulfill our preferences; however, we often overlook opportunities to do so because we are intimidated, even blinded, by the perceived effort involved. In addition, when we make choices, we may not know how to cope with the challenges that emerge before us. Freedom is accompanied by responsibility, and in fearing the journey, we might lose the treasure. In my case, I was fortunate to have psychological tools and training in my back pocket! I will share these with you so that you can also move in the direction you desire. Skills and tools are important for keeping you sane as you persist along the way.

I have combined the best advice from the multitude of popular self-help books with widely used and researched psychological principles to help you unleash your passion for life. I've learned that just a few steps are essential on the journey: get back in touch with yourself and accept who you are, learn to think rationally, create a positive metaphor for yourself, and figure out how to choose and resiliently walk upon your unique path.

You may put up many blocks for yourself, knowingly or unknowingly. You may even be doing this right now in the way you receive this book, though I hope that this is not the case. Some examples of blocking include procrastinating; being overly critical; jumping to conclusions before you have all of the information; not putting your full heart into something that could help you; failing to acknowledge the truth; succumbing to unhealthy choices; forgetting to plan actions that you know you'd better do; ignoring signals from your mind, body, and surroundings; and closing yourself off from your life through fear and pessimism. So, while it is a healthy desire to be able to follow your heart, it will make it easier if you can acknowledge your current blocks and begin to work toward removing them.

I've figured a lot out along the way, with much credit going to Dr. Albert Ellis for creating Rational Emotive Behavior Therapy (REBT). When I started to apply what I learned from REBT in a way that fit my life, I developed a seven-step system that has been useful to my clients and me. While aspects of this model have been researched and found effective, the grouping of these ideas still requires scientific testing, so I don't want to imply that this is the only way to gain relief and increased passion in your life. However, this is a methodology that I've found very helpful and, more importantly, easy!

With practice and continued use, my seven steps can set you on a course that will lead to greater fulfillment, personal gratification, and ongoing life enhancement.

One more word about freedom and responsibility: You and I are living in a time that is filled with opportunities and traps, possibilities and devastation, dream fulfillment and defeat. Before we can even start upon a personal journey, it is good to take a step back to unearth choices that may be obscured from view.

When I was at a recent book conference, a taxi driver delivered me to my hotel late one night. He told me that he liked working nights because he was able to have his days free for other things. He asked why I was there. I explained that I was a psychologist and that I was writing a book about listening to your heart and following your own path without forgetting to think rationally.

As I was speaking to the driver, he wiggled in his seat, appearing a little uncomfortable. He said, "What irritates me about self-help books is that they don't realize how much circumstances play a role. I mean, what are you supposed to do when your life doesn't allow for all of that?"

"I understand your concern, because I've seen some people in pretty bad circumstances. There are times when life is extremely hard, when you might not know how you're going to make it. There are times when you feel that you don't have enough control over what happens to you or you're going through so much that you don't know how you'd ever find a way to change things. Yet in most cases, if you just hold on long enough, eventually there will be a choice point. Perhaps the choice might only be what you allow yourself to focus upon; if you're lucky, you might have more freedom than that. Like you—you've chosen to work nights because it suits your lifestyle better."

"Yeah. I even made the choice to drive a cab. I worked in a high-stress computer systems position for twenty years. I was the one who all of the employees went to when their computer systems weren't working. The employees acted like someone was about to die when their systems went down—then they'd act like it was my fault. I felt trapped behind the desk all day."

"Well, you decided to do something very different to get a different result in your life, didn't you?"

"Yeah, now I'm out and about! To tell you the truth, I love it. People are usually a lot nicer to me in this job, I make about the same money, and I'm actually a lot happier now, even though it has its moments."

"So, you took control when you had a chance to make a choice—you listened to yourself and figured out a way that worked for you. Now you're happier. That's what my book is trying to encourage people to do, while showing them an easy way of doing it."

Just as that driver did, you had better meet one condition before you start changing your life: take ownership and responsibility for how your life turns out, even when you can tell that it is going to be an uphill battle and you'd rather blame everyone else. Consider that some of the most insightful writers of our time have emphasized the role of personal responsibility. In the *Success Principles*, Canfield's first principle is taking 100 percent responsibility for all the outcomes in your life. The ever popular media psychologist Dr. Phil says that you can't own it if you don't claim it. In *The Road Less Traveled*, M. Scott Peck also placed personal responsibility at the top of the list of variables that determine your life's outcome.

You live in a time when freedom is not a luxury, yet there are many more opportunities than ever existed before. In order to take advantage of your freedom and your own potential, you had better learn to recognize your choices and your power whenever these are present; then you can own these opportunities and seize all that is within your influence.

This is not to imply that your decisions should become self-centered or unethical, or that special circumstances are to be totally ignored! It's important to consider the gifts you already have—family, physical health, financial health, etc. If you acknowledge these responsibilities, you'll have an easier time focusing upon your own goals, enjoying the rewards your efforts will produce, and freeing yourself to grow further than those who pretend that they have none. When my mother used to buy me a new dress, she'd tell me to go hang it in the closet. If I didn't, she'd say, "Why should I get you anything else if you're not going to take care of what you have?" That would motivate me to hang it up!

It's really simple: Start by taking care of the gifts you already have in order to open yourself up for more. Brush and floss your teeth, eat right, exercise, drink water, give your children as much love as you can, listen to your life partner, and take care of what you've already got going.

This seems especially true when there are others who are presently depending upon you for their well-being (such as your children, sick loved ones, or elderly parents). I'm not saying that you have to be the caretaker for every person in your life, and with the help of this book you'll probably determine where you're going to draw the line. I want you to own your power, take care of your gifts, and adopt an ethical stance in your relationships with others.

This is one of the many paradoxes at work in life. In the process of accepting an ethical stance toward others, you'll become open to taking an increased ethical stance toward yourself as well. You'll begin to realize how making room for yourself in your own life can create more room for abundance. You'll see that as you allocate small portions of time to think, make space, and make commitments to yourself, you will gain efficiency, which ultimately saves you time and heartache. Finally, as you invest energy to following through on your plan of action, you'll gain the dividend of increased energy and power.

In order to choose to follow your strongly desired path, it is important to be rational. Dr. Ellis talks about "*must*urbation," which is when we tell ourselves that *things must* be a certain way, that *we must* be a certain way, and that *others must* be a certain way. You can drive yourself insane "*must*urbating"! Instead, it is much saner to begin to walk upon your path enthusiastically and to realistically handle things, others, and ourselves as they actually are.

Almost always, you'll face balancing acts that will challenge your progress. These will involve various forms of sacrifice (time, effort, energy, and money). In almost every case of triumph, a tale of perseverance and frustration precedes the success story. Once you accept that there is a price to pay for results, and that things frequently don't happen exactly as you desire, you will be able to enter into your life's purpose (which you'll select and create) with your eyes open and your heart encouraged.

Knowing this, I'm going to encourage you to look for ways to choose your own path *ethically* and with integrity, so that when you face frustration you will be at peace with the effort that it takes to push past it. I'm going to encourage you to be patient with yourself and your circumstances, even if it means that sometimes you move through the steps ahead very slowly. That being said, I would like to invite you to learn about the Seven Steps!

Chapter Three
Understanding Inner Guidance
The SMART Way

The *inner guide* is referred to by many terms and the source is debated as well. The inner guide is often best understood as "the still, small voice within" that coaxes us to approach or avoid, depending upon what is in our best interests. Some believe that this inner voice is divinely inspired by a higher power; others believe it is a metaphysical aspect of universal wisdom, springing from positive and negative energy; others view it as intuition; and still others believe it is each person's unique internal guiding element, basic to an individual's biology. This book does not attempt to confine you to using the term inner guide; I'm just using it for the sake of simplicity. I'll also refrain from defining the source of this process, because I believe that each person is entitled to define this for him or herself. This book is here to encourage you to honor yourself by tapping into your inner guidance system, regardless of how you define it. As you do, you will tap into a plentiful source of wisdom, creativity, motivation, direction, and clarity!

After I describe my idea of SMART Inner Guidance, I will explain how to tune in and use it by employing my seven step plan. They are the essence of what I've found to be important to becoming centered and to living a happier, more fulfilling life. I have distilled them from my years of practicing with patients, supervising interns, hearing students' stories, attending seminars, reading, learning, and creating awesome outcomes in my own life. I want you to be able to take the path of least resistance, and I want to hand these to you *now* so that you can act now. There is a lot of advice out there (and some of it is bad advice). I'm trying to distill the best of it for you into seven easy steps. Any one of these chapters taken alone would add to your life. Put them together in combination, and you have an easy, powerful toolbox that you can use to help your life take off in some incredible new directions!

In the sections that follow, I'll define what I mean by certain phrases and terms, and explain how my plan will use and fuse two great systems.

Inner Guidance and Rational Thinking

I've combined two seemingly contradictory systems of thinking into a third system, which I call SMART Inner Guidance. In order to understand what this is and how to use it, you'll need to have an understanding of the basics of each traditional system.

What do people mean when they refer to inner guidance? In general, when people refer to inner guidance, they are referring to a style of living, decision making, problem solving, and self-awareness that involves becoming quiet and turning inward for clarity. As you turn inward for answers, you'll experience various forms of communication with your healthiest inner self, what I'll sometimes call your "inner guide."

While opening yourself to your own experiences, you will probably notice that information comes to your awareness in various forms. Sometimes, you are activating many parts of your brain, so don't be intimidated by the format of the answers. Think of it as renewing a friendship with your long-lost best friend. It is as though that loving friend wants to make sure that you get the message that you're loved. So, she sends you an e-mail saying she admires you, then she sends a card that says you're super, then she sends a photo of both of you hugging, and then she sends a CD about friendship. In this renewal, you get an abundance of messages, all in different forms. So, when you get answers in different forms, just realize that it is often a normal part of the process. Here are some examples of what your experience might include:

1. Noticing an internal loving, healing, honest, and growth-promoting voice

2. Visualizing images that represent aspects of the solution to your problem

3. Experiencing initially puzzling thoughts or ideas that later turn out to have great relevance to you (kind of like a dot-to-dot picture where the dots are initially unconnected, and later seem to connect into an obvious image)

4. Discovering that you're singing a song or humming a tune that relates directly to your current problem or solution

5. Remembering dreams that are related to a question that you are attempting to address; sometimes these are lucid dreams, meaning that

you actually know you're in the dream and attempt to influence the events

6. Experiencing a strong sense about something, an intuition, a gut feeling, or an inkling

7. Feeling pulled in a certain direction, and only feeling congruent or at peace with yourself when you follow this direction

8. Being drawn to focal messages, aspects of conversations, objects, or images that seem to confirm or reaffirm an idea.

What is Rational Thinking and what are the three types of questions? Rational thinking, at its core, is sane and healthy thinking. Ideally, rational thinking allows you to think more sanely, feel healthier feelings, and make wiser decisions. However, part of rational thinking is the acknowledgment that you are fallible and are constantly making mistakes—including thinking errors. So, don't feel badly if you're not perfectly rational all the time. Fallibility is a part of being human!

Three widely used methods can help us easily decide whether a thought is rational. I think of these methods as a spam filter for sick thinking. Just as we filter out unwanted e-mail, so, too, can we filter our thoughts using the three powerful questions that I'll teach you in chapter 4. Each question is basically a test for rationality, and requires a "yes" answer to pass through the rational spam filter.

What if you answer "no" to any of the questions? In that case, the thought that you're considering is not rational. Sorry to break the news to you! But, don't despair! First of all, it doesn't have to be rational, but it would certainly be optimal if it were. It is up to you to decide how important it is to meet that criterion before you take action. Rational thought is almost always healthier to follow than irrational thought, but there are exceptions to every rule. In the event that you find your thought isn't rational, and you'd prefer to have a rational answer, simply revise the thought or return to it later with a fresh outlook. (You'll learn more about how to do this as the book continues.)

What is Rational Emotive Behavior Therapy? In 1955, Albert Ellis, PhD, developed a form of therapy known as Rational Emotive Therapy. This form of therapy developed into what is now Rational Emotive Behavior Therapy and largely created the foundation for the development of Aaron Beck's Cognitive Therapy.

There are many aspects of REBT, which has evolved into a philosophical stance as well as a body of therapeutic techniques designed to embody this stance. One of the tenets that I have found to be important and useful is that you can train yourself to think in a more rational and healthy way. Why am I encouraging you to seek healthy thoughts? Simply because these are the thoughts that lead you to make wiser decisions, take positive actions now, accept yourself unconditionally, accept others unconditionally, and feel better! Remember, everything that is ever manifested begins first in the mind. So, we'll work to clean up your irrational thinking!

What is SMART inner guidance, and how does it differ from other therapy models? SMART inner guidance combines the two awesome ideas I've just been talking about: inner guidance and rational thinking. Have you ever noticed how combining two great ideas can lead to an extremely powerful third idea—an idea that takes care of the weaknesses of the first two? Well, you're sitting on the front row of this chemistry experiment, and you're about to learn how to combine these two agents to get a third one that is out of this world! I will explain the value of this combination more in a little while.

Why is the inner guidance literature of today grossly insufficient to help you over the long term? The inner guidance literature of today is often beautiful and poetic because it encourages you to listen to the healthiest, highest part of yourself. Believe me, I love reading it. It is fun and can really help give you short-term relief. But it is inadvertently selling you short. While I have great respect and appreciation for what it offers, I have noticed a vacuum. You know that nature abhors a vacuum—well, this vacuum is just waiting to be filled, and I want to make sure that we fill it with the right thing.

Let's look at some of the problems and gaps in the inner guidance literature, so you understand why we need to go a step further. If you decide to turn inward for answers and you're not knowledgeable about rational thinking, this is what could happen:

1. You might assume that if you feel uncomfortable about something, it is the wrong direction for you. However, sometimes a period of awkward discomfort is necessary as you gain mastery over a new skill.

2. You might incorrectly believe that if you feel unhappy about something, you are taking the wrong path in your life. However, sometimes unhappiness is a signal that some element of your walk upon the path requires renewal, adjustment, or updating, rather than a complete change of course. For example, Dan left his wife and kids because he felt unhappy in his marriage. Rather than working on it, he abandoned his family,

leaving them heartbroken and confused. The decision was in response to unhappiness and the belief that unhappiness meant he should take action to get away from the pain. Had he taken things a bit further, using what you're about to learn, things might have turned out differently. It is possible that he would have asked great questions, quickly put the answers through the rational filtering technique that I'll teach you, and come up with a healthier option, such as therapy, divorce mediation, or divorce; the way he left was very damaging to his family. Just remember, anyone's decision making, even yours, can easily become self-centered and unethical if you think that all resistance and frustration is to be avoided.

3. You might make impulsive decisions rather than thoughtful ones. If you believe that you are listening to your inner guide and that the guidance you receive is telling you to do something, you might take immediate action without thinking it through. You might accidentally fail to consider your other options or the potential consequences of the option you're picking. While it pays to be decisive, impulsive decisions can be costly or lead to substandard results. For the cost of just a few extra minutes of thought, you can make smarter life decisions.

4. Some inner guidance literature suggests that there are "false" voices or "outside" voices, which can be discriminated by the fact that they are critical. This premise assumes that our thoughts are not always our own, and that critical thoughts are always false or created outside of us. While this contains elements of truth, it oversimplifies how complex our thinking process can be. Why do I say this? You see, we are endowed with the ability to think about our own thinking, what psychologists refer to as metacognition. When we think about our own thinking, we sometimes become critical of our own ideas. This usually leads us to refine our conclusions. For example, I might say, "That idea wouldn't work out just yet," or, "I'm going to have to work on getting support for that idea or it won't work." These types of negative thoughts do not have to be unhealthy and toxic for us, if we understand how and when to use them. At times, critical thoughts can be tools to help us strengthen our positions. Critical thoughts are not always self-critical, and don't always lead to dire outcomes. They can, in fact, lead to essential growth! The key is to apply these thoughts when you're in an intellectual mood, rather than in an emotional one.

5. Much of the inner guidance literature today tells us that the experience of fear is a signal that we are turning away from our true selves and from inner guidance. While I am an advocate for courageously focusing ourselves upon potential positive outcomes and for taking healthy risks, we once again have an oversimplification on our hands. Not all fear is bad and unhealthy! Fear is simply a signal, sometimes wrong and sometimes right. If fear were not somewhat adaptive, it would only be a vestige; that is, it would not have strongly survived the process of evolution (or, if you subscribe to creationism, our creator would not have given us the capacity to experience it). When there is actually something that you had best avoid, fear is a healthy signal to you to stop immediately and fight or run. Biologists call the biological response to a fear stimulus the fight-or-flight response.

Stephen Chandler, author of *Seventeen Lies That are Holding You Back and the Truth That Will Set You Free*, tells a story about a strong sense of fear that he felt during a time when a serial rapist was terrorizing entire families in his community. The perpetrator had escaped the authorities, and the community was on alert. One night Chandler woke up gripped with fear. He walked his house with a baseball bat, experiencing the strong sense that someone was looking through his windows, walking around his property; Chandler wanted the person to see him courageously ready. The next morning, as he drove from his house, he noticed police cars. When he stopped to inquire what had happened, he learned that the perpetrator had struck again. The victim was a nearby resident who had been victimized minutes after Chandler had awoken and guarded his own house. Chandler believed that his healthy fear helped to protect his family, and was shaken to hear that the perpetrator victimized someone else minutes after.

Healthy fear, which we might also call concern, can also prevent you from entering into situations you'd best avoid, and it can help mobilize you to take immediate action in dangerous situations. It would help you make the decision to avoid a certain trail when you're hiking. It might motivate you to lose weight when your doctor tells you to do it or you'll face a heart attack in the next month. Healthy fear helps you to choose whether or not to walk through a gang-infested neighborhood on your way to a restaurant and whether or not to take random risks. Healthy fear (or concern) simply serves to protect you in these instances. If you are hesitating at such moments, your inner guide is serving you and helping you to protect yourself.

This is not to be confused with unhealthy fear. This type of fear holds you back and prevents you from taking growth-promoting risks. Many speakers and writers use the letters of fear as an acronym for "fantasized experiences appearing real" or "false education appearing right." When you apply the Seven Steps, you'll learn to tell the difference between healthy and unhealthy fear more quickly and more easily.

How is this book different? This book is designed to help you by pulling together information from different schools of thought and combining it. It takes the strengths from one idea and uses it to compensate for the weaknesses in another, and vice versa. Together, this powerful combination will help you to develop your ability to turn inward for guidance and then filter out the garbage. You don't want a spam filter that is filtering out messages you need, you want one that is updated and more advanced; this system is like that, teaching you how to access your inner guidance and filter out your inner spam!

Also, this book is different from some of the others out there because everything is reduced down to seven uncomplicated yet key steps. After you read it and apply what you learn, you'll be able to use this method over and over again, with success. What I call the rational filtering technique is really based upon time-tested ideas that are at the core of self-understanding and adjustment; in fact, the same questions (which I also call the sieve of sanity) are used by many psychologists as they treat their patients. I'm going to share it so you'll have a method for becoming self-directed and self-reliant.

Finally, this book addresses the question of listening to your heart, versus listening to your mind. Since the 1700s, at least, authors and poets have portrayed the battle between the heart and the mind. Listening to your heart is a wonderful credo, and you can do this in a way that also makes use of your intellect. This book will show you how you can tap into both your heart and your mind for maximum benefit. It is a true self-help book, because it will give you the skills you need to access that which you already possess.

Using this book will help free you to start taking action toward the life you want. This book is designed to unleash the best in you and help you to start taking action right now. As you read about concepts, you will be given stories to think about and exercises to put into place right away. The ideas and techniques in this book are based upon ones that I've used with patients to help them take action and move toward creating the lives they want. When you are working toward that which you want, you will notice that you are more passionate about your life!

Learn to use a multipurpose plan of action to greatly improve the odds of your success. Because this book is organized into seven steps, the plan toward success is already laid out for you. This plan is multipurpose and multiapplicable. You can use these steps to seek answers about existing questions, refine your thinking about matters that are troubling you, or tap into your creative source. You can use these steps to free yourself when you feel blocked, and you can use them to strongly propel yourself when you are already in motion toward your goals. Once you've mastered the skills in this book, it will take just minutes of daily self-time to keep it going. Little hinges turn big doors: a few minutes of regularly targeted reflection could lead to major breakthroughs in your life!

How is Part II organized? Each chapter that follows introduces you to a single step, and each step draws you closer to tuning into your own inner guide. The chapter starts with the wisdom and rationale for the step you're reading and moves you toward a strategy to help you develop the target skill further. Sometimes the chapter will provide identity-protected case examples, scientific research backing, or an experiment or exercise to help you further own the ideas and then put them into action.

Each step is designed to help free you from unhealthy emotional blocks as you become more tuned in to what you want, and more turned on to your life. As you master each step, you will see that the process is shockingly simple and can be applied with ease throughout your life, as long as certain basic conditions are respected.

Although each step is discrete, the steps are holistic, symbolically uniting the heart, the mind, and the body. As you will soon recognize, Steps One through Four will open you to your heart, in that these steps focus on helping you return to yourself (including your purpose and dreams). In the same light, Step Five will involve your mind, in that it helps you to apply your intellect in an efficiently targeted fashion to the answers you'll receive. Finally, Steps Six and Seven involve your body, in that they guide you toward taking specific action. It is my belief that, when you unite these symbolic forces of the heart, mind, and body, you will strategically unleash your inner genius and rapidly propel yourself toward amazing outcomes.

Chapter 4 will focus on the first step toward accessing your inner guide, what I categorize as acceptance. You will work on accepting yourself, others, and situations in order to create a healthy and resilient attitude. Such an attitude is helpful in quieting the mind and opening the heart to your inner guide, not to mention in helping you to own what is in your control. Chapter 5 will teach you how to relax, how to increase your self-awareness, and how to tap into your wisdom through a variety of techniques that integrate the various parts of your brain. Once you feel accepting and relaxed, you will be open and ready to learn. Chapter 6 will teach you to turn toward your inner guide by asking questions and opening yourself to the various forms that answers might take. In chapter 7, we'll turn to the importance of recording your answers for further reference and later thought. Chapter 8 will teach you to put your answers through a rational filter/sieve of sanity. This filter is made up of some of the questions that are used by clinical psychologists educated in REBT. You'll learn what I think are the three most critical ones for clarifying whether your thoughts are rational and healthy, or whether they might benefit from tweaking. The rational filter is a way to get instant feedback on your thoughts. Once you've determined what is useful to you, chapter 9 will help you to take action, enhancing the effect through affirmation, visualization, and synergistic visualization. Chapter 10 will remind you what you've learned and give you some ideas about how to create regular times for renewal.

Is this plan a substitute for professional help? Though the techniques that I'm teaching you are designed to help you feel better and give you an option for approaching life more sanely, this book is *not* a substitute for formal mental health treatment. If you have a clinical condition, and if you are in need of care, I strongly recommend that you get proper help (psychological or psychiatric). However, many people find that incorporating the right type of self-help reading into their therapy can enhance the effectiveness of their treatment. In addition, following the completion of treatment, good self-help books (combined with *action*) can help keep you on track.

Part II
Seven Steps to Tune In and Turn On!

Chapter Four
The First Step: Acceptance

Always fall in with what you're asked to accept. Take what is given, and make it over your way. My aim in life has always been to hold my own with whatever's going. Not against: with.

—Robert Frost (1875–1963)

Acceptance is the first step along the road to SMART inner guidance. Although it may initially elude you, I hope that this chapter will help you to understand why acceptance is a desirable philosophy to strive toward. Acceptance provides the foundation upon which you will build successful passage to your healthy inner voice.

To start, you'll first decide whether or not you practice acceptance in three key areas of life. Then, you'll learn about the disadvantages of a philosophy of non-acceptance and the advantages of a philosophy of acceptance. You'll be learning why acceptance is essential for the practice of turning inward for answers, and, finally, I'll give you ten tips for becoming more accepting and strengthening what I call your Triad of Acceptance. I'm extending the ideas of Dr. Albert Ellis, who has said that the key to psychological health is "steadfastly accepting" the self, others, and life conditions.

Let's start at the beginning and assess your level of acceptance of yourself, others, and life conditions. Here are some questions to help you to begin to determine if you practice acceptance or not.

Self-Acceptance

1. Do you criticize yourself constantly?

2. Do you think that you're worthless because you lack some desirable qualities or characteristics?

3. Do you notice the negative in yourself far more than the positive?

4. Do you put yourself down for your appearance, intellect, social abilities, lack of money, inability to do something, or other reasons?

5. Do you have periods of time during which you hate yourself?

Other-Acceptance

1. Do you find yourself feeling constantly angry or enraged at others?

2. Do you wish others would just shut up, hurry up, pay up, or simply get out of your way?

3. Do you find yourself continually wanting people to act differently than they generally do?

4. Do you have periods in which you lash out at others?

5. Do you have periods in which you feel deep disappointment in others, or even hatred toward others?

Life Acceptance

1. Do you think life has given you a raw deal or that things weren't supposed to turn out as they have?

2. Do you constantly worry that things won't turn out exactly as you want them to?

3. Do you get angry at having to deal with hassles, such as having to wait in line, drive in a traffic jam, wait extra time at an appointment, deal with multiple things breaking, change plans, or send your food back due to an error at a restaurant?

4. Do you tend to have a hard time letting go of things, throwing things away, or moving on?

5. When things don't go according to your design, do you find yourself raging to others? Do you think you could be a rage-aholic?

These are but a few questions that are designed to tap into your ability to accept yourself, others, and situations. If you find that you answered yes to many of these questions, you probably have *not* been practicing acceptance. Non-acceptance can lead to many problems, as we will see in a moment.

For now, however, let's look at these three areas of acceptance, and what non-acceptance in even one area can mean to your life and to your ability to turn inward.

The three areas of acceptance are self-acceptance, other-acceptance, and life or condition acceptance. I call these the Triad of Acceptance. It will be much easier for you to turn to your inner self for guidance if you first practice strengthening your Triad of Acceptance. Your Triad of Acceptance positions you to being open to your ideas and to figuring out how you'll implement them in reality.

The influence of acceptance on inner guidance compares to the power of acknowledging that there is water in an ocean, and appreciating that this water has its own rhythm. Theoretically, if a man could enter the ocean without acknowledging the existence of the water and waves, he'd find himself confused, frightened by, saddened, or even angered about the resistance and commotion he'd encounter. If he instead accepted the circumstances of the ocean, he'd swim through it; he'd quickly find that he was tapping into the assets of the water, and becoming energized by its buoyancy, using its momentum to his ultimate navigational advantage.

Now that you understand how powerful acceptance can be to your ability to turn inward, you might think more carefully about your own level of acceptance in these three domains. Some of you might wonder what would happen if you have good other-acceptance but poor self-acceptance. You might be the type of person who says, "It's okay if they're that way, but it is not okay if I'm that way." You might think that your accepting attitude of others is sufficient, and that you can continue to be hard on yourself because it doesn't affect others. While it is good that you accept others, it is equally important that you work on accepting yourself. Remember that if any one of these three areas of acceptance is compromised, the other two will also suffer. For example, if you hate yourself, you're going to be less likely to accept shortcomings in others and in situations. Each area influences the other.

If you fail to work on acceptance in each area over the long term, you'll be more likely to develop what psychologists call psychopathology or mental illness. Whether or not you have a biological predisposition to psychopathology, you're greatly increasing your risk of it if you decide to throw acceptance out the window. Let's see how this can happen, and then you'll understand why acceptance is crucial to asking and receiving inner guidance, and how to develop it.

In terms of understanding the psychopathology that can result from lack of acceptance, I'm going to discuss what I call the Big Three: rage, anxiety, and depression. These are rampant in our current times and are often *elective*. Yes, you may unknowingly choose to suffer with these psychological ailments much of the time—that is surprising to learn, isn't it? What's even more shocking is how easily we forget what the stakes of nonacceptance are. Let me be plain: the stakes are high, folks. So, let's look at some of the possible products of nonacceptance and a few potential consequences of holding on to them. (There are also specific thinking patterns that arise with nonacceptance, such as awfulizing, low frustration tolerance, and damning, which you can read more about in my workbook, *Working toward an Effective New Philosophy*, coming out soon.)

Rage. When you fail to accept situations or others over the long haul, your irritation may grow into anger and even into rage. You might think that it is okay for you to spend precious time raging and complaining about imperfections that bug you. I had a boss that did this daily, and sometimes hourly. He'd call us in one at a time and complain about the pet punching bag of the week. While that was awkward, what was even worse was when it was your turn to be the punching bag. Now, don't get me wrong here—if you've just been traumatized, you are better off talking about and working through your rage with a trained professional instead of quietly holding it in and not knowing what to do next. However, while it might occasionally be helpful for you to talk about your rageful feelings, in general it is probably *not* healthy to do this without also getting to some resolution that includes acceptance. Ongoing raging without acceptance leads to hostility and can result in cardiac conditions and other health problems. In your life it can lead to destroyed relationships, shattered reputation, and failure in your career. In your community it can lead to failed companies, harassment, hate crimes, rape, assault, abuse, terrorist acts, and murder of groups (remember the Holocaust). At a national level such hostility leads to terrorism, war, and mass death.

Anxiety. This feeling can result from the lack of acceptance of situations and yourself. If you are constantly worrying about what is going to happen and assuming that you won't have the fortitude to cope, you are leaving yourself prone to worry, preoccupation, and lack of focus. Again, such worrying can lead to a wide variety of health problems, including panic attacks, agitation, inability to take necessary risks for growth, diminished joy in relationships, and impaired functioning in your career. Larger scale effects include diminished performance in companies and weakened communities.

Depression. Depression can develop with the lack of acceptance of the self, others, and situations. Though it is not always obvious, you can greatly contribute to depression in others if you are constantly critical of them and their efforts, especially those who are vulnerable to irrational thinking (such as children). More obvious is that you can develop depression within yourself by putting yourself down and criticizing your actions as you do them. This is a pretty sure way to get depressed, and if you do it long enough and hard enough, you may even become suicidal. This is to caution you to be aware of the possible results if you decide to self-down or put others down. If you don't have depression naturally due to a neurochemical imbalance, this is the formula that creates it! Depression can lead to death; there is no doubt about it. This death can be slow if self-hatred causes you to adopt unhealthy behaviors, or it can be racing fast if you become suicidal.

Now that you know that lack of acceptance leads to problems, let me tell you what can happen when you start working on acceptance.

More often than not, you're going to feel freer. You see, when you work on acceptance, the by-product is freed mental and emotional energy. The energy that you've been using to feel rageful, panicked, and depressed is freed for other things. When you experience freed energy, you begin to look at possibilities and potentials. You begin to set goals and work toward them. And best of all, you begin to value the present and the life you've been given. Then you'll want to make the most out of your time by using it to work toward ethical dream fulfillment rather than waste.

And when you do feel badly, it will look something like this: Instead of rage, you might feel annoyed or irritated, and that might motivate you to ask assertively for what you want, or work toward forgiving another. Instead of anxiety and panic, you might feel healthfully concerned and so you'll deal with the concern instead of being immobilized. Instead of depression and devastation, you might feel sad now and then, but you'll simply feel it. You might cry, but you'll move on, rather than lying in bed and giving up on yourself. Can you imagine the powerful implications of acceptance on your life, your career, your relationships, and even in your communities and countries?

Acceptance of the self, others, and conditions allows you to release yourself. Acceptance can thereby lead to improved ability to turn inward for guidance.

When you want to turn inward for guidance, novel things might happen. You might have silly thoughts, scary ideas, or weird sensations. When you accept yourself, you let these enter and you let them exit until you have gotten to that for which you were searching. Self-acceptance is a very desirable quality to develop in order to better tolerate the mysteries of this process.

When you desire inner guidance, you might be facing challenges in your relationships with others. When you inwardly accept others, you can receive answers that are not tainted by wanting to do harm to others or wanting to act out of anger, jealousy, or hatred. Instead, you will seek actions that create a *long-term win-win* outcome for all involved; this is the basis of *ethical decision making*. And you will be receptive to this type of inner guidance above that which creates destruction and pain in both the short and long term.

When you turn inward for guidance, you might find yourself distracted by something that happened during the day. Your energy and focus might be affected by this, but with life acceptance, you will let this go and move on with your inner work.

"Okay," you're thinking. "I'm sold on the idea that it would be good for me to work on accepting myself, others, and life's situations. But how do I do this?" There are five points about acceptance and the notion of unconditional acceptance that will open you to your accepting abilities. To make it even easier, I'll also give you ten tips to build and maintain a strong Triad of Acceptance.

First, in order to open yourself to the idea of acceptance when you're feeling nonaccepting, I've found that it is helpful to ask yourself, "What about this is in my control, and what is not in my control?" When you ask this question, it often focuses you upon that which you can change and that which you presently cannot change. The simple act of recognizing the difference often helps you to shift your focus and release the energy that is wrapped up in the area of that which you cannot change.

Second, you can begin to understand the difference between acceptance and liking something. Just because you accept something as it is does not mean that you like it that way. I accept that I have osteopenia, a bone condition that precedes osteoporosis. I don't like it, but there is nothing I can do about the fact that this is my present diagnosis. What I can do, now that I've accepted it, is to look at my options from here. I can figure out a plan of action based upon what I consider my best options, and then I can implement the plan and get regular feedback from my doctor. So, just because you accept something, it does not mean that you like it, or that you would wish for it to be that way. Because you don't control the universe, very often things won't be exactly as you'd prefer for them to be, but it is far easier to accept them and move on!

Third, it helps to understand that acceptance is not the same as resignation. Resignation means that you are giving up, that you think something will never change, and that therefore you will not try to make any improvements. Acceptance, on the contrary, means that you recognize that what is just is, but that it may not always be as it is today. Acceptance thereby mobilizes you to have the energy to work toward change because you are not stuck trying to change that which you cannot, and you begin to focus upon that which you can change.

The fourth point to opening yourself to the idea of acceptance is to make your Acceptance Triad *unconditional*. Unconditional acceptance means that under any condition, you can see and acknowledge that what is just is. You can recognize that you don't control all aspects of life, others, or yourself. Moreover, it means that you can accept people (including yourself) without liking everything about them or the things they do. So, if your spouse is acting rudely to one of your friends, you might not like his behavior, but you can accept him as a human being with flaws despite his crummy behavior! Instead of thinking, "He's a worthless, crummy person," you would instead think, "What he's doing is crummy." The same would apply to you. If you'd done something that you considered wrong, you'd define the behavior as poor, rather than yourself. Instead of saying, "I'm no good," you'd instead say, "It is no good that I did that." In the case of a shabby situation, you might say, "This was shabby," rather than saying, "Life is shabby." You would let go of forecasting the future of your whole life, and look at each situation separately.

What if something in your life is just not fair? Obviously, in an extremely poor situation, it can be challenging to accept what is. Remember, however, acceptance is different from resignation. Acceptance is the starting point for freeing yourself to determine what you want to do or think about next. Situations may be very bad, and people may act very badly, but nonacceptance leads you down a nonproductive road of blaming, complaining, and shutting down. Would you rather shut down, or acknowledge what is and then rise to the challenge?

How would you approach this type of challenge with unconditional acceptance? You might strive to improve the situation, knowing that just getting angry about it isn't going to change a thing for you. Tina's ex-husband forces her and her children into custody battles every couple of years, despite the fact that she's repeatedly proven her wonderful mothering abilities and her children voice their desire to stay with her. Tina not only does not like this situation, she is financially impaired by it every time. She has two general categories of choices: the choice of nonacceptance, or the choice of unconditional acceptance.

When she chooses nonacceptance, she becomes angry and enraged. She might spend hours on the phone crying in frustration or even planning ways to get even; however, the cost of this stance is that her overall coping is compromised, and the benefit is—well, there is no apparent lasting benefit.

If she chooses unconditional acceptance, she can allow herself to feel sad and annoyed in reaction to the inconvenience of another custody battle, but she would accept that this is the crummy reality of her particular situation and prepare herself and her children as best as she can. At some point, Tina might be in a position to become politically active and work to modify the injustice that she and others experience from what she views as financial abuse. As you can see, neither response is actually changing the reality of the present situation, but the second response helps Tina remain mobilized and cope more successfully.

The fifth and final point to opening yourself to acceptance is this: As you unconditionally accept yourself, others, and conditions, realize that acceptance is a process. It is ongoing. Don't worry if you're not perfectly accepting, just notice when you aren't and work on it. You can accomplish a lot by simply asking yourself, "Am I accepting what is?" Keep it going, and you'll feed your tendency to be accepting. Like a plant, acceptance needs ongoing sunshine, water, and nutrients to thrive.

Now that you are much more open to turning your areas of nonacceptance into acceptance, I'd like to give ten tips toward strengthening your Acceptance Triad. Do these to become more accepting, and you'll also improve your ability to be receptive to your loving inner voice—that still, small voice within that keeps guiding and urging you toward your healthiest path.

1. Know your target. Review the description of unconditional acceptance and envision what it will be like for you. Imagine yourself accepting yourself, another, or an unpleasant circumstance. What will this look like, feel like, or sound like? Develop an idea of what you are striving toward. When you know your target, you know where to aim!

2. Remember the advantages and disadvantages of aiming at your target by reviewing the costs of nonacceptance and the benefits of acceptance. This will keep your motivation high!

3. Acknowledge that life is full of challenges and each person has his or her own. Accepting that challenges and resistance are a part of life doesn't mean that you're going to be leaping for joy over them. However, you'll be more likely to simply expect and deal with resistance and move on. In addition, when you acknowledge that others also have challenges, you will loosen your demands upon them, making you more accepting of them as human.

4. Work to forgive others for being human, for struggling, for messing you up, and for imperfection. By definition, humans are imperfect and will

therefore struggle, make mistakes, and inconvenience each other all along the way.

5. Work to forgive your own imperfections. No matter how much you might want perfection in yourself, simply wanting it won't automatically make it so. Striving for perfection in yourself can lead you to vacillate between feeling nervous about disappointing yourself (and others) and feeling chronically disappointed in yourself. Does that sound like fun? Instead, strive for other goals, such as ongoing achievable improvements in a skill, and gradually work toward larger goals or dreams. By doing so, you will release yourself from the insanity of perfectionism. Progress, not perfection, is the new mantra toward life success.

6. Practice the "Garcy Bare Minimum Theory." This might be a hard one for you workaholic types, but it actually works great. I discovered a long time ago that if you consistently do the bare minimum that is necessary for good results, you will often achieve greater results than you anticipated or than others who are doing the same thing. Often, it is when you try to do too much that you burn yourself out. There is a famous Spanish expression: *Poco a poco andamos lejos*, or, "Little by little, we walk far." Experiment with this theory and let me know if it works for you!

7. Remember that the world doesn't owe you, and be grateful for your blessings. People tend to adopt two primary attitudes. The first is what I call the *brattitude attitude*. This attitude assumes that the world owes you. It leads you to feel offended when life isn't acting in accordance with your grand plan, and sometimes leads to adult temper tantrums. The second is what others have called the *gratitude attitude*. This attitude assumes that, in general, the universe owes you nothing. If you have this attitude, you're usually grateful for the blessings or good events that do occur. A gratitude attitude helps decrease misery and increase joy. It is a *choice*.

8. It all comes down to—drum roll, please—*you!* You are the one who creates your attitude (thoughts + feelings), you are the one who chooses your response to others or life, and you are responsible for creating more of what you want now. I recently heard a high school athlete on a talk radio show say it this way: "I've gotten myself into this rut, so I guess I'm going to have to get myself out of it."

9. Give up on being rescued. No one else can create life changes for you, though if you're lucky, others may support you. They might give you pep talks, might listen to you whine (which isn't really to your advantage), might give you encouragement, might offer you suggestions, or might even direct you to information that can change your life. However, you are the only one who can decide to take new information and use it. You are the only one who can implement new ideas, and you are the only one who can actually make your attitude and behavior change. Seek supportive individuals and thank them wholeheartedly, but realize that persistence and tenacity are still up to you to adopt.

10. Go climbing! Creating a strong Triad of Acceptance is like climbing a mountain: it can be tough and steep at times, and you might not realize how beautiful the view on top will be as you are hiking. Just as when you hike up a mountain, it is important to be realistic about what it will take to make it up, and about the possibility of tripping now and then. As in mountain climbing, you might realize that sometimes working on acceptance is just plain tough. It is a gradual process, and sometimes it can take time to get to your desired destination. So, in essence, I'm encouraging you to accept the challenge of acceptance. Estimate the difficulty of it for you, given the role models you've had and given how new a skill this is for you; then guess what you might need to prevail over the challenge. You might find people who've climbed the hill you're about to climb; often these people can give you hints about what you might do to be successful in your climb—sometimes they even leave stakes in the ground as they go, which you can use to pull yourself up the hill. Other times, you might find people to help you take off the blinders so you can see your path more clearly. These helpers can include therapists, coaches, support groups, and friends who are there to help you make it up that mountain more easily.*

*Because I believe in people optimizing the help they seek, I want to invite you to access a free download about benefiting from therapy. I created this as a bonus gift to you, to help you save time and money. Simply log onto www.myinnerguide.com/free_gift/. I believe that the download contains fabulous time-saving information to help you have a great therapy experience!

Chapter Five
The Second Step:
Relaxation and Flow

Two men look out a window. One sees mud, the other sees the stars.

—Oscar Wilde

Yesterday morning, I went into my bedroom to tell my husband something that he needed to know about the day ahead. When I entered, he happened to be jogging on the treadmill and watching the television news. He had turned the volume of the news all the way up so he could hear it over the noise of the treadmill. It was pretty loud in there! Slightly shocked by the noise, I started speaking very loudly in competition with the treadmill and the television. Then, as he seemed unmoved by my message, I tried yelling it, but he only gave me a confused look in response. It could have been part of a sitcom because it was really ridiculous. I finally had one of those "aha" moments that Freudians talk about, and I recognized that I'd better ask him to turn down the volume of the television! Magically, he turned it down and was able to hear, understand, and respond to what I was trying to say.

What happened yesterday morning is actually a great metaphor for listening to your own inner voice—you know, the one that is trying to enlighten you and urge you to respond, but you're just not able to hear because of all of the interfering noise in your head? If you are going to be able to listen to the softer, more rational voice that is trying to break through to your consciousness, you have several choices. You can wait until the mind or body's signals are *screaming* at you, or you can just allow yourself to turn down the volume of all of the chaos, chatter, self-doubt, and self-criticism that prevent you from moving forward.

In order for you to turn up the volume of your healthiest inner voice, this chapter is going to focus upon the skill of relaxation. It is a skill, like any other. It can be learned, you can improve with practice, and there are always new ways of enhancing the effects that you are achieving.

When you learn to relax, you can allow yourself to be more open to your internal experience. There may be times at first when you feel nothing from relaxing. As you proceed, you might notice that you simply feel more physically relaxed. Over practice and time, you might feel more refreshed and focused mentally. Eventually, you may learn to relax until you feel rejuvenated, energized, and ready to take on your next challenge.

People often stop working to develop their ability to relax for two reasons: fear and lack of patience. However, because you've already started working on self acceptance, these hurdles might dissolve more easily for you.

Let's address the first hurdle: fear. It is normal to feel some fear before trying something new. After all, you don't know what the process will be like, and you don't know if you're going to have a negative experience. Your fear is simply serving to protect you from harm. However, in almost no instance will the process of relaxation harm you. In fact, it has been found to promote health and to enhance quality of life. Even if the only thing you learn from this book is to relax, you will be better off than when you started. Therefore, you don't have to feel badly about feeling fear, but you can reassure yourself that many people have relaxed successfully and have attained positive results. It is very likely that you can, too!

In addition, I've found that many people find it helpful to have permission to relax only as much as they feel comfortable relaxing, and to stop whenever they see fit. So, based upon this, you can give yourself permission to stop at any time during your relaxation exercise.

Another type of permission that might reduce your fear is the permission to have whatever experience you have, and to eliminate the demand that you must become a relaxation guru in one or two attempts! Any experience is okay, if you approach it with acceptance. While you are relaxing, you can tell yourself that any thoughts or images you have simply reflect your unique style of traveling from where you are into a more relaxed state.

In this regard, it is all right if the fear has not passed and if you continue to feel it as you start your relaxation exercise. You see, for you, fear may be a phase that you pass through prior to relaxing. This fear may be of losing control of your emotions, of not knowing what might happen if you allow yourself to relax, or of new internal experiences you assume might be unpleasant. Susan Jeffer's book, *Feel the Fear and Do It Anyway*, shows that it is okay to feel fear and then push past it. *You don't have to push past it all at once; a little at a time is okay.* But pushing past it can lead you to achieve the growth you naturally desire. Remember this: if you are feeling fear, it is often simply a sign that you are moving outside your comfort zone.

A ship at dock can travel nowhere. Release the anchor that keeps you tied at dock; allow yourself to travel, explore, learn, and grow. You are still in control of the ship and you can always return to dock if the waters are too rocky for you. You can at least test the waters; think of what wonderful experiences you might have!

Now let's address the second obstacle: lack of patience. As you'll see, this obstacle is one of irony. Put simply, this is because the more impatient you are with yourself, the longer it will take you to relax. You actually disturb yourself about relaxing (leading you to feel anxious) when you impose an arbitrary time limit or an unrealistically high standard to your practice. The longer it takes you to learn to relax, the longer it will take you to get to Step Three of *The Power of Inner Guidance* (and believe you me, you don't want to skip Step Three), and the less likely you'll be to tap into this wonderful supply of wisdom that you've been carrying with you all along. I want you to have great results and I want to help you dissolve these obstacles so you can move forward more efficiently. Believe it or not, you'll probably make more progress if you take your time learning to relax. Take it at your own pace. Sometimes, if you tell yourself that this is going to take however long it takes, and remind yourself that rushing things may actually slow your progress, you'll relax a bit just from that freedom. You really aren't losing anything by taking as long as it takes to learn how to help yourself. If you are impatient by nature, then be impatient about getting started, and get started learning right away. But, after that, tell your impatience to wait in another room while you're relaxing! Remember, once you learn to relax, you'll have it for future use, through thick and thin. As Oliver Wendell Holmes once said, "A mind once expanded by a new idea never returns to its original dimensions."

Do you have other reasons for not relaxing that don't fit into these two categories? Contact me through my site, www.myinnerguide.com, and I'll work to address your reason in my online newsletter. However, since we've addressed these two main obstacles, I think you're probably ready to learn the skills you need to relax. I will teach you some that have worked time and again for my patients and for me!

Learn to relax and observe. There are many paths to the same destination. I am going to introduce you to one; however, if you have another method of attaining a calmer state, feel free to use it instead.

Before you start, make sure that you have a private and safe location (never in a moving vehicle or while operating heavy equipment, of course), that you have uninterrupted time to practice (don't answer the phone or door), that noises around you are pleasant or nonexistent, and that the temperature in the room is comfortable for you. Soft lights and calming colors such as blues and greens can enhance the effect you're working to achieve. In addition, essential oils such as lavender can be calming. You can purchase lavender at the health food store and place a drop into the melted wax of a burning candle (not the tapered kind). This way, the scent of lavender will fill the room. Alternatively, if you are not allergic to it, you can place a drop into some unscented lotion and rub it into your skin.

After you've addressed the setting and your blocks against relaxing, you need to learn three fundamental techniques. The first is breathing, the second is muscular release, and the third is observation. All are done in an atmosphere of acceptance. Let's turn to each one, and then I'll provide you with a script to use to get started.

1. **Breathing.** Diaphragmatic breathing means that when you inhale, your stomach rises while your chest stays very still. When you exhale, your stomach falls and your chest stays virtually still. It is as though a balloon in your belly inflates with each inhalation and deflates with each exhalation. This type of breathing differs from chest breathing, which is a rapid type of breathing that you might see during a fight-or-flight response. Some people find that, if they inhale, hold their breath for a second, and then exhale, they become more aware of whether or not they are breathing diaphragmatically. Once you've shifted your breathing to diaphragmatic breathing, work to slow your breath. Count how long it takes you to inhale and then count how long it takes to exhale. See if you can gradually increase the amount of time it takes by two to three seconds. If it takes you three seconds to inhale and three to exhale, see if you can increase this to five or six seconds apiece.

2. **Muscular release.** Mentally scan your body for any areas that might feel tight or tense. If the area is injured, mentally imagine the surrounding muscles releasing any tension, and then allow yourself to release the tension for real. If the area is not injured, you may tighten the muscle, hold for a count of three, and release the tension. Notice the difference between the relaxed muscle and the tense muscle. Now release all other muscle groups in the same fashion. As you note the differences between tension and relaxation, you are teaching yourself how your muscles feel when relaxed. In doing so, you are becoming more aware of how much tension you have been holding in your muscles.

3. **Observation.** Observe yourself, your breathing, the way that you are holding your body, and how your body feels when it is relaxed. Observe the space around you, including the temperature, any sounds, any scents, and the feeling of your body against your bed, floor, or chair. Observe anything you see around you. Observe the thoughts coming into your mind, and simply allow the thoughts to leave as they came. Observe your breath going in and out. Notice the improved feeling of calmness that is beginning to pass over your body and mind. Enjoy this feeling. Focus yourself on the here and now. The past is history and you cannot change it now. The future will wait. Focus on the now, the only thing that you truly have before you. To enhance your relaxation, use the Self-Awareness Sentence Starter, a technique I started using early in my training. Read it to yourself as you mentally fill in the blank. Repeat it several times to become deeply present-focused and accepting of the now.

The Self-Awareness Sentence Starter:

I am aware, here and now, of _____.

Case example: Hannah was an elderly woman who suffered from panic attacks that began following a car accident. She was forced to pass the accident site on her way to various places that she frequented. When the thought of the accident entered her mind, she'd start to feel anxious. When she felt anxious, Hannah would become very worried about feeling this way and would work herself into a panic-stricken state. In addition to learning to accept herself for feeling anxious and to accept life conditions for having dealt her this accident, Hannah benefited from learning to relax. She started by learning to breathe deeply and slowly. Then, she learned to relax her muscles. Finally, she started becoming more present-centered and self-aware by continuing to fill in the blank in the Self-Awareness Sentence Starter. As she became aware of her senses, and aware of the present, she was able to release the strong grip of the past and calm herself so that she could then live her life in the present.

Allowing yourself to reconnect and recenter involves an openness to a variety of experiences. As you connect with yourself, you will relax more deeply, and as you relax more deeply, you will connect with yourself. It is the essence of a healthy cycle. Below I will discuss some ways to further connect with yourself and to turn on to your experience. I'll introduce you to the ideas of *flow, vital absorbing interest,* and *self-expression* below.

Mihaly Csikszentmihalyi's best-selling book, *FLOW: The Psychology of Optimal Experience,* talks about enhancing the quality of your life by entering a state of total absorption in what you are doing. Csikszentmihalyi says:

> Flow helps to integrate the self because in that state of deep concentration consciousness is unusually well ordered. Thoughts, intentions, feelings, and all the senses are focused on the same goal. Experience is in harmony. And when the flow episode is over, one feels more "together" than before, not only internally but also with respect to other people and to the world in general.

Learn what allows you to flow. It may be that to enter a state of flow, you might benefit from relaxing first and taking a small step toward your passionate pursuit. Simply allow yourself to take the next step when it is natural for you. If you find that you are absorbed and flowing, losing track of time, allow yourself to continue to enjoy the experience. When you have a healthy passionate pursuit, it will intrigue your mind fully and you will become more mindful.

Pursue or figure out what Dr. Ellis calls your "vital absorbing interest." This is the healthful thing that absorbs you, fulfills you, leads to long-range rewards, and is something you want to spend more time doing and improving. It is what Jack Canfield calls your "core genius." It is the activity that calls you, draws you to it, wakes you up, captivates you, and that you feel passionate about doing. You also feel satisfaction as you do it, and you enjoy your natural mastery of it, wanting only to improve upon it. As you pursue this interest, you will find that you are able to connect more fully to yourself and to your healthy inner being.

Self-expression may also allow greater self-connection. Music, dancing, singing, chanting, writing, painting, poetry, art, cooking, loving, and other forms of self-expression are like buttons on the remote control of your consciousness. Each button leads you to a different channel that you may view, understand, and later return to. Each time you view another aspect of yourself, you will be able to understand yourself more fully. As you understand yourself more fully, you will be better able to make decisions that are in alignment with what is right for you.

Chapter Six
The Third Step:
Ask and Receive

Direct your eye inward, and you'll find
A thousand regions of your mind
Yet undiscovered.
Travel them and be
Expert in home-cosmography.

—William Habbington, quoted in Henry David
Thoreau's, *Walden*

Now that you've learned how to start working toward self-acceptance and you've learned how to start relaxing, you're ready to learn Step Three. However, I would just like to add a caveat: for optimum results, you will need to continue to practice Steps One and Two. Although you may have already achieved greater self-acceptance and you may feel great relief from learning to relax, you will be able to maintain these gains by making them a part of a daily routine. Now that you've experienced the initial impact of using these two new tools for improving your life, you can probably understand the importance of continuing to work on mastering these skills. If you have a low Triad of Acceptance, you will certainly want to work on this aspect of yourself throughout the day. I recommend that the lower your Triad of Acceptance is, the more frequently and regularly you practice. In addition, if you have had long-term challenges relaxing, you'll probably want to practice this skill to enhance calm and positive feelings and to develop a stronger self-connection. There are many books and tapes on relaxation, and you can go to my Web site (www.myinnerguide.com) to download an audio-relaxation exercise for further practice.

That being said, I don't want you to think that you have to be perfect in these areas in order to make progress on Step Three! I just want to encourage you to keep up your good work. Now, let's help you get to Step Three!

Very simply, I call Step Three "ask and receive." Step Three is actually the crux of becoming self-guided, because this is when you will start to get answers to your daily questions, as well as to the larger questions about your life.

Here is the overview: You'll determine if the timing is right. If it is, you'll start by doing Steps One and Two. That is, you'll work on accepting yourself, others, and conditions, and then on relaxing yourself. Then, you'll turn inward and ask yourself a specific question (more on how to do that in a moment). You'll quietly observe the answer you receive. Often, you will hear your healthy inner voice responding back to you. When this is the case, you will experience it as honest and supportive, rather than globally critical. This will be the time to record your answer (Step Four), which we'll get into in the next chapter. However, there are times when the format of the answer is different, as discussed previously. For example, you might have a visual image of a place, accompanied by music. Experiencing the answers in different ways is common, but these different modes can be fruitful if you attend to their symbolic meaning.

After this, you'll progress to Steps Four, Five, Six, and Seven. You'll want to know when and when not to do Step Three, so here are some tips for increasing the effectiveness of your experience.

DO: *Wait until you're in a neutral or positive mood before starting Step Three.* If you are in an extremely dark and gloomy mood, I recommend you work to improve your mood, using some of the suggestions below, before you start turning inward for guidance. Otherwise, the answers to your questions are likely to be tainted with your own self-downing statements, as well as with pessimism, cynicism, anger, and negativity. Instead, you want to elicit your healthy and helpful inner voice, which will include self-statements of support, acceptance, possibility, and potential.

DO: *Address negative moods through positive actions so that you can return to Step Three.* Assuming that you've ruled out a physical cause for your mental state, you can often work through it. Positive actions often help relieve a temporary negative mood. It may be that you need a break and that getting out of your current environment for a little while would help. For example, Mona, a stay-at-home mother of four who frequently turns inward for answers, finds it helpful to go outside for a break. She once confided, "Simply going outside and looking at the clouds in the sky, observing the trees, and listening to the birds can be very leveling." Spend a few minutes being rather than doing. Others find taking a walk in nature, connecting with friends, switching tasks, doing something kind, or taking another positive action can help them out of their momentary melancholy.

Another positive action you can take is to learn to challenge your irrational beliefs. In *How to Stubbornly Refuse to Make Yourself Miserable About Anything, Yes, Anything,* Ellis discusses how to talk to yourself at such low points. He says, "Whatever you *choose* to do, you can also *refuse* to do." In order to improve your feelings, it is often helpful to look at the thoughts that preceded them and then decide whether to choose to think other thoughts that might be more helpful. By challenging yourself about whether what you're telling yourself really fits, you'll open yourself to the possibility of healthier, more rational ways of thinking about your situation.

One easy technique used by most REBT and CBT therapists is to start distinguishing between situations (which are neutral), thoughts (which can be rational or irrational), feelings (which are the labels you give to your emotional states), and behaviors (which is what you do in response to your thoughts or feelings). You can use this technique as well. Simply by distinguishing between these different levels of experience, you are gaining deeper understanding of what is driving you to feel a certain way: your habitual ways of thinking. Then, you can decide whether you'd like to revise what you're thinking to a thought that is more helpful and healthy, more evidence based, and more logical. Sometimes, you might even see humor in your irrational thoughts, which will help you rise above them and think through things differently. For example, depending upon where you are in this process, you might be able to joke around with yourself by asking, "Do I think that the universe has to respond exactly as I specify?" REBT emphasizes that the thoughts that disturb us most contain absolutist shoulds, musts, and have-tos. These terms can be used in an arbitrarily demanding fashion (which is unhealthy), or in a conditional fashion (which is healthy). For example, an absolutist thought (unhealthy should/must) might include a statement such as, "I must have all of my work done." Alternatively, an example of a conditional statement (healthy should/must) might be, "I should get my work done if I want to get paid." Conditional statements have a condition associated with them. Absolutist statements are arbitrary and often unrealistically demanding.

This process has many names, such as cognitive restructuring, the triple column technique, and challenging irrational beliefs. Regardless of what you call it, when you're first starting to use it, it really helps to write things down. This places everything in front of you so you can see it and think about it with more objectivity. Therefore, I've provided a place for you to do this below. You can also click on the link on my site that takes you to an REBT Web site to complete an online self-help form, which contains similar components as those on my table. Many authors have developed variations of the form that I'm sharing below (including but not limited to David Burns, Michael Edelstein, and Windy Dryden). However, I've also added a few of my own qualifying questions at the beginning; these are designed to help you to target your work more effectively.

Feel free to make copies of the Bad Mood Box below and use it whenever you're in a bad mood.

Bad Mood Box

Observe your answers to these questions, then answer the questions that follow:

1. I'm in a bad mood. ____true _____false

2. I accept this in myself. ____true _____false

3. Even if I accept this, I would like to see if I can change it. ___true ___false

When all three are true, you're ready to work on the feeling you're having right now. Proceed to the questions below.

If any of the above questions are false, it means that you probably have a barricade to working on your bad mood.

When the second question is false, you're probably condemning yourself in some way or worrying about the fact that you're in a bad mood.

When the third question is false, you might be seeing your mood as out of your control, you might not want to do the work involved to shift it, or you might be blaming someone else for your bad mood.

So, if you have a barricade to working on your bad mood (such as feeling angry about feeling sad, feeling anxious about feeling angry, or feeling scared about feeling scared, etc.), please start your work below with your feelings about your bad mood. Once you've worked to eliminate the barricade, do the box a second time, focusing upon the primary bad feelings (overly sad, overly angry, overly scared, etc.) on the next part.

Using single-word descriptions of your emotions, list your feelings.

_____

_____

If you were an impartial news reporter, how would you describe what happened before these feelings emerged?

_____

_____

What did you say to yourself about this event?

_____

_____

_____

What did you end up doing?

_____

_____

Look at what you said to yourself. Was there an absolutist thought (should, must, etc.)?

_____

What evidence do you have for or against your thought?

_____

Just because the situation occurred, does it follow that your idea must be accurate?

_____

Are there other explanations?

_____

How helpful is it for you to hold onto this belief?

_____

What would be a better way of looking at things?

_____

_____

_____

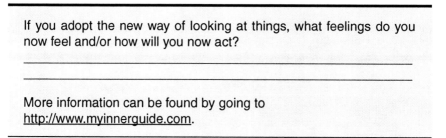

If you adopt the new way of looking at things, what feelings do you now feel and/or how will you now act?

More information can be found by going to http://www.myinnerguide.com.

Figure 1: Bad Mood Box

As you can see, the effectiveness of this method of improving your mood lies in helping you make decisions about your thoughts and gain greater objectivity. Then you can revise unhelpful, overly negative, and irrational thoughts until you get to a thought and philosophy that you can ethically buy into and use to create rational feelings (which don't feel as bad and aren't as disruptive to your life).

Douglas Bloch's book, *Listening to Your Inner Voice*, suggests yet another method for helping yourself during these down moments. When you turn inward and all you get are negative answers, you can create an affirmation to respond to them. He calls this type of conversation with the self an "affirmation dialogue." Whenever you have an area of lack or limitation, rather than dwelling upon it, Bloch suggests creating an affirmation of the way you would like it to be instead. For example, if your relationships are challenging, you might create an affirmation that says, "I am attracting open and loving relationships." By saying this to yourself, you begin to trigger the brain to attend to an alternative to your current perception. Affirmations are best used in a repetitive, ongoing, and routine manner (for example, every morning and night). They are also best stated in the present tense, as opposed to the future or past tense. This way, you can trigger a stronger response that is easier to step into.

In addition to affirmations, visualization and mental rehearsal can also be helpful. When using this technique, you envision yourself in action, easily doing that which you've been wanting to do, be, or have. If you've wanted to stop smoking, you can visualize yourself saying, "No, thank you," when someone offers you a cigarette. If you've wanted to behave more assertively, you can imagine yourself confidently and calmly expressing your preferences. If you've wanted to have financial success in your life, you can visualize yourself reading about money, learning about money-making strategies, accepting money, saving money, and investing money.

If you've tried the suggestions above and you still feel crummy, stop and think for a moment. Evaluate your Triad of Acceptance (Step One). Often, you'll find that you are not accepting yourself, others, or conditions—you might benefit from further work on this. Or, you might be very wound up from the stress of the day; you might benefit from relaxing (Step Two).

DO: *Find or create a quiet, calming place for turning inward.* If you don't already have a quiet place in your house, start by creating one. Some people create a clutter-free corner or a sitting room just for inner work. Cool, soft colors, such as blues, turquoises, and some greens, are often soothing.

DO: *Take advantage of the fact that you are a sensual creature.* Tap into each of your senses to help yourself relax and focus upon the now. You can use aromatherapy and add the essential oil of lavender to the melted wax of a burning candle. A few drops of lavender essence mixed into your body lotion or dabbed on your pillow case can help you tune into your present moment and your senses. You might try some herbal teas, which are designed to help the body relax. At other times you might enjoy the simplicity of sitting and drinking a glass of water, attending to its temperature and consistency as you slowly sip it. Fragrances may have deep associations for you that lead you into a calm and happy state (for example, occasionally baking a special family recipe will fill your house with a homey smell, which you may find very comforting). Certain foods may be associated with calm and comfort in your life (soups, stews, and various comfort foods); you might consider keeping these on hand as a special soothing enhancement. Homeopathic remedies can be used to create relaxation and improved concentration, depending upon what effect you are hoping to achieve. Music can enhance and deepen your experience; try softly playing Mozart's symphonies or nature sounds in the background. Others prefer to notice silence or tune in to repetitive sounds (such as the sound of the washer and dryer, the sound of a clock ticking, or the sound of a tranquility fountain). Still others find the tactile support of water to be especially soothing. Sara found that, when her husband died, her swimming pool became her special place. She swam daily to re-center. Margaret felt that after a stressful day she was best able to meditate while in a hot bath with the lights of her bathroom off and a lavender candle flickering near the mirror. Keep in mind that not everyone responds in the same way to the same stimuli. Robert found that when he sat in front of his computer and breathed deeply, he was most effective at relaxing and turning inward. Simply by sitting in front of his computer, he felt comfortable, competent, and at ease, which helped loosen him and improve his openness.

DO: *Condition yourself to turn inward in your special area.* This is easiest if you have one or two special places where you go only to turn inward. While you can turn inward anywhere and at anytime, turning inward in a specific location will begin to trigger an automatic response. When you begin to create such a routine for yourself, you will notice that your body begins to relax and your mind begins to focus more easily. Day by day, this pattern is strengthened through repetition. While some days will still be easier than others, you may find it valuable to think of this as inner guidance hygiene in which you use a certain spot only for this practice (not for distractions such as watching television, talking on the phone, etc.).

DO: *Keep a method for recording insights handy.* Usually a simple notepad and pen work great! When you read the next step, you will learn more about the importance of this.

DO: *Start by relaxing fully.* Tension and negativity often create barriers to awareness. As you relax more and more deeply, these defenses start to melt away, opening you to the abundance of possibilities that are waiting to be revealed to you.

DO: *Patiently ask yourself one question at a time.* Sometimes your questions will not lead to answers. This is fine and does not imply failure. Asking questions is somewhat like planting seeds in a garden. The seeds will require time to germinate and grow before they present their flowers. Just as a seed may invisibly grow below the surface, your questions may invisibly initiate mental processes that will bear fruit at a later time, perhaps in your dreams or in your thoughts weeks later. Know that the simple act of asking will get you closer to your answers.

DO: *Start turning inward with open-ended questions.* Remember, many times we have the answers right at our fingertips if we will only take the time to access them. Just as a computer yields specific types of answers when specific types of searches are entered, your internal search will also yield specific types of answers based upon the type of search. The type of searching you do is determined by the types of questions you ask. *What* and *how* questions are very useful for identifying problems and solving them. For example, you can ask yourself, "What can I do to about ___?" or, "How can I ____?" *Why* questions often yield answers that will help you to gain greater self-understanding, such as, "Why am I blocking myself?" However, there are times when *why* questions lead to defensiveness; if this occurs, simply rephrase your question to a *what* or *how*. *Who* and *where* questions can help you determine resources to turn to for more help, such as, "Who wants to help me?" or, "Where can I go to find that?"

DO: *Recognize the power of* how *and* what *questions.* While you do not need to limit yourself to *how* and *what* questions, it is interesting that these two categories are especially helpful. When I interviewed Donald Meichenbaum, PhD, named one of the ten most influential psychologists of the twentieth century by *American Psychologist,* he noted that expert therapists tend to ask more *how* and *what* questions. They do this because these lead to responses that establish your responsibility over your own life and empower you to take action. Asking "How can I do this?" or "What do I need to consider?" can lead to your most powerful answers!

DO: *Receive answers with respect and gratitude.* Be grateful that you are capable of receiving information, and that the information from which you may receive answers is abundant. People are sometimes too quick to judge the answers they receive, thereby shutting themselves off from the process. We might not like what we know to be true. However, think of it this way. If you did a computer search and a specific set of answers emerged, you might be disappointed, but you would accept the fact that these were the answers. In the same way, when you receive answers from your inner guide, accept that these are your answers at this time. Simply accepting this reality can be a very powerful first step to helping yourself.

A principle known as Ocaam's Razor says that the best solution to any problem is usually the simplest. Apply this principle to your own searching. Keep it simple. Ask your questions simply, and receive the simple answers that follow as though you were opening a gift. When you posture your attitude in this fashion, you will be open to receive! Good luck, and on to Step Four!

Chapter Seven
The Fourth Step: Record

No problem can sustain the force of sustained focus.

—author unknown

An old expression has it that the palest ink is superior to the strongest memory. Turning inward on a regular basis certainly represents an improvement to ignoring yourself. However, if you really want to make use of the information that you are learning, you will find it important and pragmatic to start recording your answers, so that you will truly be able to sustain your focus, approach your answers carefully, or return to them when you are of a different mind. This chapter will discuss some methods for recording your answers, it will enlighten you about the variety of formats your answers may take, it will provide some reasons why recording your answers will benefit you, and it will provide some suggestions about how to utilize the information before proceeding to Step Five. Once you've read and understood this chapter, please record one of your ideas to use in Chapter Eight.

Starting to record your answers can be simple. The two easiest ways to record your answers are manually and verbally. If you record your answers manually, you might want to keep a notebook and pen next to you as you turn inward. Alternatively, you might want to keep your laptop turned on and near you, ready for use. Whenever you ask yourself a pertinent question and receive an answer, go ahead and write down or type whatever answer you receive. If you record your answers verbally, simply speak your answers into a voice-activated tape recorder. Keep this recorder available whenever you plan to turn inward so that you can immediately input your answers. The advantage of using a tape recorder is that many folks can speak faster than they can write. The disadvantage of using a tape recorder is that if you want the answers in a visual format, you'll have to return to the tape recording and write the answers down (or have someone else do this for you).

You can try both taping and writing down the answers you receive from turning inward.

Once again, remember that the format of answers can vary. It is helpful to take a stance of the grateful recipient as we learn, receiving all gifts, however different they may be, with graciousness. You may receive answers in many forms if you are open to this experience. Most commonly, people hear a wise or nurturing voice within themselves answering the questions verbally. However, some people find that they start to hear a song in their head, that they imagine a place they've seen or see a specific picture in their mind's eye, that they are reminded of a memory that they initially thought was inconsequential, or that they experience feelings.

For example, Janice asked, "How can I help my son learn?"

She got the answer, "Stay beside him," and had the sensation of immediate calm. She was not certain what this meant, but she wrote down the answer. When she returned to it later, she still was uncertain what it might mean, but she decided to simply sit beside her son as he did his homework or practiced his piano. To her amazement, simply sitting beside him created a noticeable improvement in her son's academic achievements and piano performance. She has continued this practice with great success.

Jack Canfield tells a story about meditating on the title of his book. He asked what title would be best. Eventually, he got an image in his mind's eye of a hand writing on a blackboard. It wrote the words, "Chicken Soup." He didn't know what this might mean, so he continued to ask and heard an inner voice telling him that people's souls were sick. Just as a grandmother's chicken soup often healed the body, his books could become like chicken soup for the soul. He got chills as he realized that this was his title—and the rest is history.

Others have similar stories. Richard Paul Evans tells of his experience writing his book, *The Christmas Box*, and how much of his inspiration came from an inner voice that guided his writing.

Jean Houston talks about how information can come in many forms. She discusses how various cultures communicate messages of healing to each other through music, dancing, and chanting. She tells the story of a young boy that could not solve even the easiest math problems in the traditional manner, but who was capable of solving highly complex math problems in a fashion that included chanting and dancing. Dr. Houston encourages us to be open to receiving information in various forms, as we may have potentials that are untapped simply because we limit the modalities of our expression and learning.

Why recording your answers is useful. When you accept where you are, relax deeply, and turn inward for answers, you are in a primed position: you are open and ready to gain useful information. However, sometimes people hold back in asking themselves all of the questions. They worry that they will forget the answers. How much better would it be for them to record their answers? Recording your answers helps eliminate the concern that you will forget something important.

Other times, people do not want to make the effort to record their answers because it seems like too much work. They think that because they are relaxed and comfortable, they shouldn't have to move around (to write their answers down), speak (to say their answers into a tape recorder), or disrupt the physical comfort they're enjoying. Indeed, it does feel good to relax! However, if you want comfort in the short run, you may sacrifice larger gains in the long run. There may be particular insights or pieces of wisdom that reveal themselves to you and that you miss simply because you do not want to disrupt your physical sense of comfort. To capture information for long-term benefit, recording it in some fashion is the simplest route.

One of the major benefits of recording your answers is that you can leave judgment and interpretation for another time. You can allow yourself to openly receive and capture answers in various creative formats, rather than judging them, which will help more answers to flow to you. If a judgmental voice arises in your thoughts, simply say, "You'll get a chance to judge this later." If interpretations begin to arise, allow them to either enlighten you or tell yourself that you'll think more about the meanings of this information shortly. Just as taking a judgment-free stance in a relationship allows other people to unfold and reveal themselves to you, taking such a stance in your relationship with yourself will help you to unfold and open up to hidden aspects of your personality that may have retreated from criticisms of the past.

Some suggestions before proceeding to Step Five. As you record your answers over time, you may begin to notice themes. Sometimes, turning back inward about these themes can be helpful. For example, as I started my writing, I often noticed an image of the woods with a dirt path. When I turned inward about this image, I learned that I wanted to work toward doing workshops in a natural setting.

It is helpful to ask your pertinent heart-based questions before proceeding to Step Five, because Step Five involves a more intellectual, less creative process.

However, even after you've completed Step Five, you can always return to asking yourself additional questions as they arise.

You may want to use the space below to start recording the answers you receive.

Chapter Eight
The Fifth Step: Smartly Decide

Thought takes man out of servitude, into freedom.

—Henry Wadsworth Longfellow

Congratulations on making it this far! You are doing so well! You've adopted a philosophy of acceptance, kept yourself relaxed, asked and received, and recorded your answers. You're almost there! Many of you might even feel as though you have all you need already. Let me ask you this—how could you take the information you have and go one step further with it? How could you enhance and improve upon it? Now, please select a conclusion from those you've collected in Steps Three and Four, and get ready for Step Five!

The chapter that follows will introduce you to three philosophical methods to refine what you already have. These methods are surprisingly simple questions, especially once you understand the enormously powerful and targeted impact of their answers. If you use these questions, you can evaluate the rationality of any thought and thereby decide whether to develop its power, change its form, or ignore it altogether. Psychologists have learned that the more rational the thought, the healthier will be the emotions and behaviors that follow it. The healthier the emotions and behaviors are, the less likely you will be to block yourself as you tackle the challenges before you. In addition, in my opinion, healthy thoughts are by nature highly ethical because they maintain an interest in preserving the dignity and integrity of those within their influence.

There are two additional reasons why I am sharing this step with you. The first reason is that I want to prevent you from oversimplifying to the point that you miss out on important signals that you might gain from inner guidance. I've noticed that people easily discount information that is not exactly what they want. They are prone to make excuses and ignore signs that there are changes they had better make. Contributing to this problem is that some inner guidance authors will suggest you should ignore any answer that is laced with even a hint of fear or criticism; you should consider it a "false voice," an "outer voice," or "evil."

Indeed, we are inundated with information and messages from unsupportive others, and there are times when we carry the fear and negativity of this information into our creative domain. However, while this explanation may have merit, it can also be an oversimplification that prevents us from making necessary changes.

Just as there is a yin and a yang, just as there are opposing forces that together unite to create completion, I believe that ultimate growth involves the strengthening of your ability to balance the positive and negative information that makes itself available to you. Rather than ignoring all unpleasing information, it may be better to learn a quick and easy formula for determining whether or not the information will be useful (this is what I'm about to teach you). In this way, you can discriminate between that information which creates healthy concern versus that which creates unhealthy and paralyzing fear. You can decide between that information which helps you to correct your course for the better, versus that which shuts you down and turns you off.

Moreover, if you resort to an oversimplified model, what will you do with information that isn't negative, which seems to arise from you, but which you're not sure about? Sometimes you will ask yourself a question and will get answers that I would classify as clutter. This information isn't an outer voice, a false voice, or based in evil. Rather, it is simply the excess that your brain is sifting through in order to get you closer to your best answer. In a moment, you will see how these quick questions can help you here, too.

The second reason for this step is that humans appear to have a biological propensity toward short-term gratification, which creates thinking patterns that are not always to their benefit. For example, we all know people who will find a way to justify a chronically unhealthy behavior pattern. In order to prevent this, it is helpful to have some criterion questions that override our tendency to move away from short-term pain and toward short-term gratification, over and above long-term gratification. REBT psychologists know that healthy individuals emphasize striving toward "long-range hedonism," rather than "short-range hedonism." Therefore, I find that it is helpful to be on the lookout for thinking patterns that lead us down the road of poorer choices. Especially when we allow this free-flowing aspect of the self to come into play, information tends to ebb and flow in an unrestricted fashion, much as waves move in the ocean. It is helpful to be able to use our intelligence to smartly decide which waves are most optimal for harnessing, and which are best ignored.

Now that you understand the reasoning behind these questions, I will share them with you and you can apply them to the idea you selected earlier. I refer to these questions as the *sieve of sanity*, because they filter your thoughts through a sieve, distilling and refining them so that you are left with only the most functional, rational, and ethical. This sieve of sanity is based upon three types of reasoning that psychologists use to determine whether a person's thinking is rational. These questions have been categorized in various ways and given various names. The three categories are based upon the idea that a rational thought is useful, truthful, and logical. As Ellis says, if you use a process of scientific questioning, "it helps you discover which of your beliefs are irrational and self-defeating and how to use facts and logical thinking to give them up."

The first question is the pragmatic one: Is this thought helpful or useful to think?

The second question is the empirical or truth-focused question: What is the evidence for or against this thought? Is it true?

The third question is the logical question: Does this thought have to follow from what I know? Are there any other possibilities that are equally possible or more reasonable?

Did you apply these questions to your idea? What were the outcomes? Sometimes, your idea will fail to meet these criteria. When that occurs, simply decide whether you want to tweak the idea, or whether you want to discard it. Sometimes, you can work with the wording of your thought to make it more rational, whereas at other times, the thought is best ignored.

Let's take an example. Let's say that you'd completed the prerequisite steps, and that in turning inward for guidance, you were met with the suggestion, "You could use a vacation." You could apply the three questions. Would it help you to think that? Perhaps, because thinking that might propel you to arrange for a vacation. Is there evidence for or against this idea? Perhaps there might be, if you are overworked or are running too fast, and if it has been many months since you've taken time to rest. Is it logical, knowing what you know, that you'd benefit from a vacation? It may very well be time to "sharpen the saw," as Abraham Lincoln first discussed. So, in this case, you might smartly decide to find a time and plan a vacation into your life.

Let's take another one. "You should give up." There are indeed times to give up and times to endure. You could ask yourself, "Does it serve me and others to think this?" You would then evaluate the pros and cons of giving up and determine an answer. The next question is, "Is there evidence for or against it?" You could take your time to list that as well. The final question is, "Does it follow from what I know that I should give up?" You could look at what you know and see whether any other conclusions are equally plausible. At that point, you could look at all of your answers. When they are all stating yes, you would give up; when they are all stating no, you'd best persevere.

When you put your thoughts through the sieve of sanity, you will quickly, easily, and intelligently decide whether your ideas are rational and what you will do with your ideas. Remember, there are no guarantees that this process will lead you to the answer of your dreams 100 percent of the time, just as there are no absolutes that you must follow a fully rational course of action. However, this process will help you to increase the odds that the direction you are going is life-enhancing. By definition, the more rational the idea, the more likely that implementing it will be to your benefit. By the same token, the less rational the thought, the less likely that it will be to your benefit to carry it forward.

There may also be occasions during which you have an irrational idea, but you can revise the wording so as to create a more rational idea. Irrational ideas usually come from an underlying demand-driven philosophy, rather than a preference-driven philosophy. A demand-driven philosophy is one in which your ideas are stated as dogmatic demands, often using terms such as "should," "have to," "must," and "ought to." A preference-driven philosophy is one in which ideas are stated as wishes, desires, and hopes. So if, after the preceding steps, your belief is stated, "I must speak to Dan," and you find that this belief is irrational, you could revise the wording to become more preference-oriented such as, "It would be great if I would speak to Dan." At that point, you might find that your idea better meets the criterion of rationality, making it SMART to proceed!

Finally, if you determine that your idea is irrational, you may decide that you want to return to Steps One, Two, and Three. Sometimes the act of refuting an irrational belief clears the way for healthier guidance to enter. If you find that your idea is irrational and that you don't want to consider it further, try returning to Steps One through Four.

Case example: Sheila was rejected by her sister and brother following a family dispute. In therapy she learned about acceptance, relaxation, and turning inward for guidance. When she turned inward, she asked why she had troubles with her brother and sister. The answer came: "You probably aren't loveable. That's why they don't care for you." She brought this to the session for further examination, explaining that she'd thought this way for many years. This thought had held her back from making new friends. It kept her tongue-tied when she ran into her siblings at a cousin's wedding. As Sheila learned the three questions, we first looked at the evidence for or against her idea. She recognized that she had other people in her life who loved her, and that she was indeed loveable. Then we looked at the logic behind one aspect of her belief—did it have to follow that if they didn't talk to her or show they cared, and if she had troubles with them, that she was unlovable? No, that did not have to be the case. Finally, we looked at the pragmatic value of her idea—was it helpful for her to think this way? No, it certainly was not. Sheila reported that she felt relieved and realized that she wanted to return to the process of asking herself questions now that she'd refuted this restraining belief.

Chapter Nine
The Sixth Step: Implementation

Waste no more time talking about great souls
and how they should be. Become one yourself!

—Marcus Aurelius

Look how far you've come! Bravo! By now, you've developed some ideas to guide your actions. In addition, before you started to implement the ideas of your heart, you checked in with your intellect, thereby improving the quality of your ideas further and discarding any mental clutter. This chapter is designed to help you use what you've just distilled. We are about to put your ideas into action! We'll use discoveries I've made over the past twelve years in working to motivate people to make transformations, take action, and maintain peak motivation. This chapter assumes that your idea has traveled through the domains of unconditional acceptance, ethics, and the sieve of sanity. It assumes that your idea has bubbled up to the surface and then survived these filters. It assumes that you are now ready to take action upon your idea!

And, guess what? When you take action, you not only end up closer to your desired outcome, you end up more confident in your own abilities. Guess what that does for your capacity to tap into inner guidance? It makes it grow exponentially each time you take the right actions. Like the physics law of inertia—that objects at rest tend to stay at rest and objects in motion tend to stay in motion—so, too, can you begin a life of positive action and momentum over one of inert energy and immobilization.

Now I want to share my ten greatest discoveries about promoting your ability to take all of the action you want to take!

The first discovery that promotes action is this: the bigger your idea, the more important it is to honor it. Our first instinct is to run away from big ideas—they seem too big, too unbelievable. They may even shake us to the core! But, without the courage to undertake the biggest of your ideas, you are restricted to your most mundane pursuits. Your potential can become confined to the limits of your vision unless you are willing to search for more or to be open to visionaries who can see more within you than you see within yourself. Jean Houston talks about the possible human in the possible society. She reminds us that we each have the potential to become social artists, creating solutions for the problems that face us individually, in our families, and within our communities. Ideas are the seeds and actions are the nutrients that help your ideas to bear fruit.

The second discovery is that you don't have to already know *how* to reach your destination in order to get there! When I underwent the Jack Canfield success coaching, I learned about our inner Global Positioning System. I learned that you program yourself to reach a destination simply by having a crystal clear vision of it, regularly visualizing yourself at this destination, and then routinely affirming to yourself that you are experiencing the feelings that result from your efforts. You can also use visualization and affirmation at each step along the way, visualizing yourself easily taking the next step in your plan and affirming the good feelings that are associated with the successful accomplishment of this step.

The third discovery is that you can usually use inner guidance to identify basic action steps that will move you toward your goal. Ask yourself, "What can I do to get started?" Often, you'll find that you seem to already know what to do, who to speak with, or what to learn about! Again, you don't have to know exactly what all of these steps will be. But you probably know of some beginning steps, which will eventually lead you to identifying your future steps.

The fourth discovery relates to the third: it is best for your successful action steps to represent a tiny fraction of the total purpose that drives them. For example, your ultimate purpose may be to help others, but your action steps might include giving money to a charity, helping a friend solve a problem, or visiting the elderly. In other words, the ultimate purpose behind your actions can be as large as you can possibly envision, but your daily action steps are best broken down into tiny, easily achievable portions. Cognitive behavior therapists call this chunking, because you envision all of the possible action steps that you can and then take out a small chunk to chew on. So if your goal is to turn your business into the top of its kind, you might start with the chunk of creating a successful Web site. Then, because this chunk may be too large, you break it down further into even smaller action steps (getting referrals to Web designers, interviewing Web designers, finding out what content is needed, signing an agreement, composing the content, sending the content to the designer, paying the designer, and so on). You would then pick out one chunk and work on it. Before you commit to a chunk, make sure that you can definitely complete it. Then commit to it and complete it!

The fifth discovery is one that all psychologists are taught in graduate school, yet many seem to forget with their patients! It is the simple secret of combining positive reinforcement and the Premack Principle.

Positive reinforcement is that which you apply to increase the frequency of a behavior (you get paid to work, so the pay is the positive reinforcement). An example of positive reinforcement: to increase your rate of exercise, you say that after you've exercised, you will put five dollars into a "fun money" fund. Once you've saved your money, spend it on something frivolous and totally fun. Remember that reinforcement can come in many forms, from food to fun with friends to self-reinforcing statements. If you have read the Bible, you know that when G-d created something, G-d self-reinforced by stating, "It is good." And when He was finished, He rested and enjoyed what He had created.

The Premack Principle is a learning principle that uses a high frequency behavior to reinforce a low frequency behavior. In plain English, you do something challenging before you do something you'd do all the time (eat, watch TV, etc.). An example of the Premack Principle: to increase the odds of exercising first thing in the morning, you say that you will get to take your morning shower only after you've exercised. Your high frequency behavior (showering) serves to reinforce the lower frequency behavior (exercising first thing in the morning).

Combined, these two secrets are like putting high quality fuel into an empty racecar! Start to apply them and watch yourself take off!

The sixth discovery is based upon what many of the most successful time managers employ to keep them focused on what is important. There are activities that are part of our daily schedule, which we generally do with great regularity. There are also those that are less urgent but are important to our longer-term desires. Less successful people tend to ignore those activities that are potentially enduring—they frequently use the phrase, "I don't have any time for that." However, more successful people have found that they can schedule these activities into their lives. Highly successful people tend to find a time-planning system, such as a week-at-a-glance calendar, to schedule their activities. In addition to scheduling their needed routine activities, they also regularly schedule in time to devote to their bigger ideas. What could happen if you regularly committed to your bigger ideas?

In addition to scheduling this activity into a planner, an entrepreneur that I know regularly sits down and writes out his biggest ideas on index cards. He orders these cards and tries to implement one big idea a week. In doing only one idea a week, he maintains a singular focus, which keeps him from getting over-whelmed. In addition, by writing all of his ideas and ordering the cards, he can be more exhaustive and remember all of the things he wants to do. He also gains clarity and momentum by placing the cards in order of priority, scheduling these into his planner, and committing to taking action.

The seventh discovery is to remain open to learning about you, no matter how old or expert you think you are. Start by learning about your strengths and your weaknesses. Then learn what motivates you—for example, you might be moti-vated by love, fun, peace, achievement, status, or power. Here is the very best secret about knowing yourself and using the information to propel you forward: *Once you discover your source of motivation, use it to define a purpose that drives your passion! Once you discover your personal weakness, use the opposing demeanor to over-come your obstacles!* For example, I learned in my coaching with Ken Porter that I am motivated by love—receiving love and giving love. This is the motivation that I use to drive my passion. I composed a mission statement and a statement of per-sonal purpose—this was how we began to see that love was key to my purpose and what ignited me to take action. However, I also learned about my weak-nesses, which included taking life too seriously, becoming too serious about little things, and not acting assertively. How could I move forward with such weak-nesses? As I said, adopt the opposite demeanor during times of weakness; that is, use the antidote to the weakness. So, when I started to run away from my pas-sionate pursuits because I was too serious, I would take on the persona of some-one who was fun-loving, turning whatever I was doing into a game. And when I started to shirk from taking a risk because I felt uncomfortable about behaving assertively, I would take on the opposite persona—I would act as though I were the CEO of a large, successful company and think of myself bulldozing through whatever task was before me. In this way, I was driven by my passion and main-tained my drive by employing the antidotes to my weaknesses. REBT talks about developing high frustration tolerance, and I think that this is one method of doing so.

The eighth discovery relates to another aspect of building your frustration tol-erance and ensuring progress. It is what Stephen Chandler, author of *100 Ways to Motivate Yourself*, calls the importance of routine. You can create a routine that incorporates your action steps. Eventually, it will be your practice to take the steps that are necessary to meet your goal. My husband, Roger, is a successful marathon runner. Every day, he wakes up between 4:30 and 5:00 AM, drinks his runner's drink, and runs according to a schedule developed by his coach. Once a month, he runs a race. Once a week, he runs with his running buddies. He stretches after runs and before bed. Roger has developed a routine that serves his ability to move forward in his running. His routine has become so much a part of our lifestyle that we seldom question it. Through consistently applying this routine over time, Roger has brought himself from an amateur classification to a competitive one, winning many medals and trophies along the way.

The ninth discovery, which will help you to determine what to include in your routine, is what Jack Canfield, in his book *The Success Principles*, calls the Rule of Five. I love this rule because this is what I used to start writing. The Rule of Five uses the metaphor of chopping down a tree. If you used a sharp axe to take five swings at a large tree each day, the tree would eventually come down. When I wrote my first manuscript, I used this rule and found myself making rapid progress. At first, I attempted to write five pages a day. Then, I realized that editing five pages was equally good. Day by day, I saw myself making progress toward my goal.

The tenth discovery is taking energy breaks. When I was a student, I used to drive myself like a machine. I completed my bachelor's degree in three years, and then completed my master's degree in a year. During the spring semester of my master's program, I decided to take twenty-one graduate hours of work. Although it was not encouraged by the graduate school, I wanted to get my degree quickly. I would read and work until all hours. Guess who got chicken pox a second time as an adult? Luckily, I was able to finish the master's degree and begin a PhD program that fall. But even in the PhD program, I pushed myself unlovingly. I wondered why I was so stressed out all the time. It was not until a classmate and I had a talk about the magic of breaks that I started to see things differently. She told me how much more productive she was when she took an afternoon off during the weekend and when she forced herself to do something fun after working for three hours. I found out that I was much more efficient and had a much saner lifestyle using what I now call energy breaks. I've continued to use this idea in my work, and have found that the most successful people I've worked with also take consistent breaks to refuel and regenerate between their efforts. This last discovery provides a nice transition to the final, seventh step of my inner guidance program, Rejuvenate and Return, which you will find on the next page.

Chapter Ten

The Final Step:
Rejuvenate and Return

"I feel so depleted," Harriet said tearfully as she looked out of the tinted gray window in my office. "I never get a break."

Harriet was a newer client. She worked twelve-hour days as an administrative assistant in a hospital. When she left work, she generally went straight home to cook and clean for her husband and their son.

"You sound so tired and unhappy. It is tough driving yourself so hard," I reflected.

"That's really it. I am tired. I am unhappy," she said, continuing to cry.

"What is in your control here, Harriet?" I asked, attempting to gently mobilize her.

"Nothing," she countered hopelessly. Silence. A shoulder shrug, hopeless breath, eyes cast down.

"You drove here today?" I asked.

"Yeah," she answered, still looking out of the window.

"Harriet, something just occurred to me. Does your car have gasoline in it?"

"Yeah. Even that is so expensive these days."

Ignoring the complaining behavior, I proceeded, "Do you stop to get gas regularly?"

"Yes, of course I do. I can't afford to run out of gas. All I need is to miss work and get fired."

"That's smart of you. Do you do routine maintenance on the car—you know, oil changes, tune-ups, stuff like that?"

"Every few months I take it in."

"So, you take good care of your car and it works well?"

"Yes, for the most part," she said, chuckling in bewilderment.

"I know, you're probably wondering why I'm asking all of these car questions."

"Well, yeah." She laughed a little.

"Well, when you said that you felt depleted, it reminded me of a car that had run out of gas. It was as if you were saying, 'I've run out of gas, and I don't have the time to refuel.' Am I right?"

"Yes, actually."

"What would you say to me if I told you that I didn't have time to refuel, but I was also out of gas?"

"That you'd better make the time to fill up!"

"Yes, Harriet, exactly. And, so, what would cure your depletion?"

"Making time to fill up?"

"Basically, yes. It is in your control to schedule time for yourself to 'refuel' and regain the energy that will drive you to the next destination. I'm not saying that it will be easy or convenient, but I'm saying that it is in your control."

Harriet and I then looked through her schedule. To her surprise (and relief), she discovered a variety of ways to refuel and create time for renewal in her day. In this chapter, we will use Harriet as an example as we talk about why people don't refuel. You'll learn how to prevent burnout, the power of weekly and daily time-slots, and how renewal can help you to access inner guidance.

Why don't people refuel? Why do they drive themselves so hard? Why didn't Harriet come up with the answer of refueling on her own? In psychology, we often use the phrase "vicious cycle." Harriet was in a vicious cycle. She worked twelve-hour days, came home and worked some more, and went to bed. She actually worked more hours than the medical staff, who worked in shifts. Because Harriet was working so hard, she began to experience burnout. In this state, she was unable to see her options clearly and easily, so she continued to live in this fashion, and she continued to suffer. It became a vicious cycle. It is as Einstein once said—the same consciousness that creates a problem cannot be the one that solves it.

To prevent burnout and to prevent the phenomenon of becoming trapped in the consciousness of our problems, it is important to create opportunities to step outside of our daily reality. When you create a daily time-slot, you will find that you are fresher and more efficient during your day. When you create a weekly relaxation day and use the time to restore yourself, you may discover that you are actually more productive than you would have been had you continued at a hectic pace. Religions speak of taking a Sabbath every seven days, and universities give tenured professors a sabbatical every seven years. So the seventh step is to designate a day for rest, reflection, and relaxation at least once every seven days. In addition, scheduling a short time each day, perhaps in the morning after rest, can serve to rejuvenate you. Being that you may be very goal-oriented, you're probably thinking, "Well, what am I supposed to *do* during that time-slot?" I'll tell you.

During your weekly time-slot, the only goal is to relax and renew yourself; *be* rather than *do*, rest rather than create. You might start by sleeping as much as possible. Sleep late in the morning and take a nap in the afternoon if you can. Then, focus upon healthy intake. Drink lots of water and eat healthfully. You've now laid the groundwork for renewal, because you'll feel fresher and more receptive to life. This is a great time to take a nature walk in the fresh air or to listen to the sound of the rain. This is a great day to tell your family that you love them and spend time with those you love. This is a day to hold your son on your lap and speak softly to him, to stroke your daughter's hair, to inhale the scent of your freshly showered partner, and to give a friend a hug. Take time to listen and receive pleasure. Perhaps you will find replenishment in reading, watching a play, going to a film, or listening to a speaker. If you are religious, attending your religious services may provide fulfillment. Combining the regularity of a weekly relaxation day with the variety of life can help you to remember what this journey is really about.

During your daily time-slot, simply take advantage of outlets for releasing tension. There are two types of outlets: stress outlets and creative outlets. Stress outlets include relaxation, meditation, yoga, power-walking, aerobic exercise, kickboxing, and biofeedback, to name a few. Creative outlets can include painting, drawing, writing, sewing, baking, woodwork, crafts, singing, sculpting, pottery, and dancing. Sometimes a stress outlet is a creative outlet and vice versa. When you tap into stress outlets and creative outlets, you will find that your stress level is lower and your passion for life is higher. When your stress level is lower, your body will release fewer corticosteroids, which have been found to have adverse effects upon memory and cognition. You are actually creating a healthier environment for your brain, in addition to your body, when you create a time-slot a day.

When you relax and rejuvenate in a regular way, you will find that you are more receptive to inner guidance. Your answers will flow to you more quickly and immediately. It is as though you've cleared the way for your wisdom to rise up and emerge transparently before you. This is an opportune time to return to the self and to reawaken what has been there all along. Relaxation, renewal, and returning to the self create openness: openness to life, to your dreams, to your love, and to that which has been present in you from the beginning. This energy source is abundant and is always there for you, and you now know that accessing it entails honoring yourself and others in the process.

Lather, rinse, repeat! Once you've put these steps together, you will see how it is actually very easy to use them and apply them. The final thing to remember is to keep it going!

Returning to your inner guide will help you to remain centered, purpose-driven, and healthy. You often have all you need, if only you will seek it. Remember to listen to yourself—you may just find that the answers you're looking for have been inside of you all along. I wish you the best as you continue to grow through life in love and respect!

Epilogue

Yesterday seemed like a hazy cloud in the distance. He looked up and saw the cracks and crevices before him. Magnificent! His mind flashed back to the start of this journey.

The sound of the guide instructing him came back to him. "You'll need the right shoes and tools or you'll be slipping all over the place. You could have a serious fall. After your shoes and gear are ready, you need to learn the technique and the territory. Then, it is just a matter of trusting your instincts."

He remembered how, for the first time, he felt confident in trusting his instincts. He realized that the work he was doing—accepting himself, relaxing, turning inward, asking and receiving, writing down his answers in a journal, later evaluating them and taking action—was leading to his inner calmness. He acknowledged to himself how taking weekly time to recuperate had also contributed greatly to his newfound openness.

All of his hard work was beginning to pay off. He had gotten a new job that felt more congruent with his heart. He and his wife were working things out. It was as though he was listening to her for the first time, and vice versa. He remembered the reasons he was drawn to her, and he stopped allowing others to tell him how to live his life. He was using his inner guide to lead him through his problems instead of using others to avoid awareness.

Now, as he looked around, he recalled the climbing lessons he'd taken over the past weeks. Here he was, prepared with his climbing shoes, backpack, sunscreen, camera, and instincts. He quickly put his hand in his pocket to make sure that he'd remembered his younger brother's compass. He might need it as he ventured out. His friend was up ahead with the rope and other gear. He had set everything up and was waiting. "You go first," his buddy said.

He began the precarious climb. He watched his own hand grabbing rock as his feet methodically followed, each searching for temporary ownership of cracks or protrusions that might help propel him up the side of the glorious mountain. The weather was magnificent, and he felt the sun warming his skin in the midst of the slightly cool air. He was focused and relaxed, pushing slightly upward with his left foot, while pulling with his left hand and grabbing with his right. Up he went, passing challenges as though he were a prehistoric primate climbing a tree, and his rope were his tail.

Then, he saw it ahead: the precipice. He pulled himself up with a forceful grace that he'd never known he possessed until that moment. It was as though he'd been born to climb. He looked around, admiring the view from the summit. He couldn't help but smile and breathe in the fresh air. After several minutes of appreciation, he thought, "What now?" A voice inside said, "Search." He remembered a tip he'd gotten to look to the southeast. He took out the compass and began walking in that direction, passing around a boulder that was blocking part of his view. When he went to the other side, he saw them. There they were—in the distance, the seven peaks he'd heard about. He knew that over time, he'd get to know each of these peaks. His buddy was still waiting below. "You gonna come down?" he heard his friend shouting with eager curiosity.

"Yeah, I'm coming—I just saw the peaks!"

"Awesome, aren't they? You'd never imagine the view!"

"Yeah—I never knew! I definitely want to do those!"

"We will!" his friend yelled up from below.

He looked around once more. Then he yelled to his friend, "Okay, let me attach everything—I'm coming down."

He quickly latched the metal hook in place, grabbing the rope behind him. As he secured himself to the rock, he began walking slowly backward, his friend helping to guide him below. Then he pushed off a bit and began to rappel downward. He loved the feeling of free-falling! He felt liberated and energized! Down he came, his friend stepping back with hands out supportively. The sound of his two sturdy feet touching the soft, pale ground punctuated the moment.

"Want me to take your picture?" asked his friend.

"That'd be great!" He felt incredible and wanted to capture the moment. He knew that later that night, he'd want to show his brother the picture.

"You look like you were having the time of your life," said his younger brother, smiling. The two men were sitting at a table, waiting for their waiter to bring dinner, looking out at peaceful green hills under a cloudless sky.

"I was."

"You've really been getting into this, haven't you?"

"It's awesome, what can I say?" said the older brother as he admired the view through the large window. Then he turned rather suddenly and looked directly into his younger brother's eyes. "So much has changed since I've starting doing my own thing. It really makes a difference. Thank you for all you've done for me."

"It's just good to see you happier," said the younger brother. After a moment of quiet thoughtfulness, he said, "I'm glad you've finally discovered your passion!"

"Me, too!" laughed the older. "Oh, by the way, I need to return a couple of things to you—here's the compass, and here's the book you loaned me. They both helped me find my way!"

References

Aurelius, Marcus. http://www.qotd.org/index.shtml, 2007.

Bloch, Douglas. *Listening to Your Inner Voice*. Minnesota: Hazelden Foundation, 1995.

Burns, David. *The Feeling Good Handbook*. New York, New York: Penguin Group, 1999.

Canfield, Jack. *The Success Principles: How to Get From Where You Are to Where You Want To Be*. New York, New York: Harper Collins, 2005.

Covey, Steven R. *The Seven Habits of Highly Effective People*. New York, New York: Simon and Schuster, 1989.

Chandler, Stephen. *100 Ways to Motivate Yourself: Change Your Life Forever*. New Jersey: Career Press, 2004.

Chandler, Stephen. *17 Lies That Are Holding You Back and the Truth That Will Set You Free*. Los Angeles, California, 2000.

Csikszentmihalyi, Mihaly. *Flow: The Psychology of Optimal Experience*. New York, New York: Harper Perennial, 1990.

Edelstein, Michael. *Three Minute Therapy*. Aurora, Colorado: Glenbridge, 1997.

Ellis, Albert. *How to Stubbornly Refuse to Make Yourself Miserable About Anything, Yes, Anything*. Secaucus, New Jersey: First Carol Publishing Group Edition, 1990.

Evans, Richard Paul. *The Christmas Box*. New York, New York: Simon and Schuster, 1993.

Frost, Robert. http://www.qotd.org/index.shtml, 2007.

Garcy, Pam. *Interview of Donald Meichenbaum, Ph.D.*, http://www.myinnerguide.com, 2006.

Houston, Jean. *The Possible Human: A Course in Enhancing Your Physical, Mental, and Creative Abilities.* New York, New York: Penguin Putnam Inc., 1982.

Jeffers, Susan. *Feel the Fear and Do It Anyway.* New York, New York: Ballantine Books, 1987.

Longfellow, Henry Wadsworth. http://www.qotd.org/index.shtml, 2007.

Thompson, Lawrence Roger. *Robert Frost—The Early Years, 1874-1915.* New York: Henry Holt and Company, 1966.

Thoreau, Henry David. *Walden.* Mineola, New York: Dover Publications, 1995.

Wilde, Oscar. http://www.qotd.org/index.shtml, 2007.

Dear Reader,

Now that you've allowed yourself to access and use the power of inner guidance, it is time to ask yourself a critical question: how can I go further?

One answer might be to learn more and share what you learn with others!

I invite you to visit my Web site at http://www.myinnerguide.com. I've created this special site just for you! You can visit it to learn more about what I can offer to you, and to find suggestions for other sites to visit. You can even ask questions about inner guidance and I'll attempt to answer them in my free e-zine, *Insourcing: Inner Guidance Secrets*, which you can sign up for at http://www.myinsourcing.com.

The power of inner guidance is something you have within you, waiting to be used. It's often untapped in this age of information overload. I encourage you to create a network of supporters in the process of furthering your own inner work. As you exchange resources and learning with others in your circle, I invite you to submit your success stories to me. Sharing your growth with others will further empower you to live a life of passion!

I hope this book has served you and that I will be meeting you soon along the way.

Pam Garcy, PhD

978-0-595-42240-1
0-595-42240-3

Printed in the United States
88911LV00005B/253-498/A